Moon Garden

Moon Garden

Unlock the Secrets to Gardening
by the Lunar Cycle

Supernature

Tend the earth with patience
and honor the Moon's guidance

TABLE OF CONTENTS

INTRODUCTION

We are nature and everything is connected

G ardeners come from all walks of life, but they often share some common characteristics: a love for nature, a passion for nurturing life, and a desire to connect with the Earth in a tangible way. While it's difficult to generalize, gardening often appeals to people who are looking for a creative outlet or a form of relaxation.

In terms of demographics, gardening is particularly popular among adults who have reached middle age or older, although interest in gardening among younger adults and even children has been growing, particularly with the increased focus on sustainability and local food production.

We all come to gardening from different directions. My own pathway to gardening was laid in the soil of a 10-acre citrus orchard on the outskirts of the city. My parents fondly named our land St. Clements, echoing the well-known English nursery rhyme, "Oranges and lemons, say the bells of St. Clement's." This refers to St. Clement's Church in London, a hub for merchants dealing in imported citrus fruits. On our property, we cultivated not only oranges, lemons and grapefruit but also an assortment of produce including tomatoes, asparagus, avocados, and kiwifruit. My hardworking parents grew it all.

Years later I was introduced to organic gardening through my work in publishing and from there became a little more conscious about how I was treating the earth and the health of the environment. So, when by chance, I found an old Moon gardening calendar dated from the 1970's tucked inside a drawer at my parent's house, I was intrigued.

This book is the result of my exploration into that very concept. In the chapters that follow, we'll look into the history of Moon gardening, dating back to ancient civilizations that planted by lunar and astrological calendars. We'll dive into the science—or the lack thereof—that might explain why some gardeners swear by this method.

We'll take a look at some Moon gardening methods, such as planting by the Moon phases using a Moon calendar for gardeners. For those interested in delving a little deeper, we will look into the more complex systems of biodynamics. The goal is to offer a comprehensive and holistic framework for your garden. At times, the discussion will lean towards general strategies to enhance your organic gardening experience. However, wherever possible, the focus will be on harmonizing these strategies with lunar phases for maximum gardening efficacy.

My journey into Moon gardening has been revelatory, and as the Moon waxes and wanes above, I find my connection to the earth deepening below. This book is an invitation to join me in that dance. Together, let's explore the fertile interplay of soil and stars.

Welcome to Moon gardening.

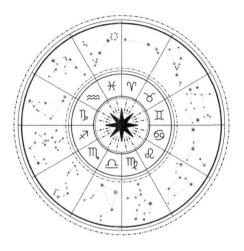

CHAPTER 1.

What is Moon Gardening?

Moon gardening is a distinctive approach that takes into account the Moon's phases and their impact on plant development. It stems from the belief that the Moon's gravitational pull, much like its influence on the tides, affects water levels in the soil. This, in turn, has implications for plant moisture, sap, soil composition, and even the water table.

The effects of the Moon's gravitational pull are magnified at different stages of its cycle. By aligning gardening activities with the correct point in the lunar cycle, proponents of Moon gardening believe they can optimize healthy plant growth, increase yields, and enhance the overall well-being of their garden. With experience and astute observation, gardeners can discern how the Moon's influence on planetary bodies significantly influences plant growth, resilience and assists in efficient task planning.

At its core, Moon gardening involves attuning oneself to nature's rhythms—the sun, Moon and stars. As we delve deeper, we discover that these natural rhythms can be harnessed to create harmony and well-being in other aspects of our lives. Connecting with the Moon's phases taps into our inher-

13

ent desire to be in sync with nature.

Gardeners who undertake planting, cultivation, harvesting, weeding and other garden tasks during the appropriate lunar phases report substantial improvements in the flavor, yield and vitality of their edible crops, all without the need for additional fertilizers. This outcome is good on so many levels, from saving money to the improved taste of your produce, your personal health and the overall well-being of the planet.

Moon Gardening reaches back to antiquity

Planting by celestial cycles is a practice that reaches back to antiquity, woven into the fabric of agricultural traditions across civilizations. This is not merely folklore or the stuff of old wives' tales; it's a deeply rooted form of knowledge that has been observed, refined, and handed down through generations. Some might say it's an ancient wisdom that has been largely overlooked by modern agricultural science, but it is experiencing a resurgence as researchers dig deeper into understanding its principles and efficacy.

One of the earliest known Moon calendars tailored for agricultural practices was probably written by Hesiod around 800 BC. Hesiod, a Greek poet, wasn't just spinning verses; his works provide crucial insights into the agricultural methods and celestial timings of his era. Fast forward several centuries, and you encounter Pliny the Elder, a Roman author whose *"Natural History"* serves as an encyclopedic record of ancient knowledge, including agricultural practices. In his writings, Pliny covers a myriad of topics, from animal husbandry to the proper times for planting and harvesting, often tying these activities to lunar cycles and celestial events.

Historical figures like Cato the Elder, a Roman statesman and agriculturalist, and even Francis Bacon, the Renaissance philosopher and scientist, have also contributed to this corpus of knowledge. Cato's works include practical advice on farming, laced with observations on how lunar and planetary cycles affect plant growth. Bacon, known for his methodical approach to scientific inquiry, questioned and examined the traditional lore to separate superstition from empirical fact, yet he did not entirely dismiss the influence of celestial bodies on agriculture.
14

Now, let's delve into the fascinating life and work of Sir Jagadis Chandra Bose, a pioneering scientist from India who lived between 1858 and 1937. Bose was a polymath, but one of his most captivating areas of study was plant physiology, specifically the sensitivity of plants to various forms of energy.

In a time when the study of plant life was far less advanced than it is today, Bose embarked on groundbreaking research to demonstrate that plants are sensitive to minute levels of energy. In essence, he set out to prove that plants can respond to subtle stimuli, much like animals do. His work was revolutionary because it challenged the prevailing notion that plants are merely static, unresponsive organisms. Instead, Bose posited that plants are capable of complex responses, even though they don't have a nervous system like animals.

Bose utilized an array of innovative techniques and equipment to document plant reactions. For example, he developed extremely sensitive instruments that could detect the faintest changes in cell structure and movement in plants when exposed to stimuli like light, heat, or chemical agents. He also employed early versions of what we'd now call "lie detectors" to measure plant responses to various conditions. These instruments showed changes in plant cell pressure and electrical activity that indicated a form of "response" to external factors.

The results were nothing short of extraordinary. Bose discovered that plants reacted noticeably to various forms of stimuli, demonstrating that they are far more sensitive to their environment than previously assumed. This didn't merely imply that plants grow towards the light or that they have basic survival mechanisms; Bose's research suggested that plants can interact with their surroundings in a more complex, nuanced way. His work was so impactful that it laid the groundwork for future studies in plant neurobiology, a field that explores the signaling and communication processes in plant cells.

However, like many innovators, Bose faced a fair amount of skepticism and resistance from the scientific community. Critics questioned his methodology and even the very notion that plants could possess sensitivity akin to sentient beings. Despite this, Bose's work has stood the test of time. It has been increasingly validated as technology advances and our understanding of plant physiology grows more sophisticated.

While Bose did not specifically focus on lunar gardening, his research resonates with the concept. His work implies that if plants are sensitive to localized stimuli like electrical currents, they could also be attuned to larger cosmic rhythms, such as lunar cycles. Thus, Bose's pioneering studies indirectly validate the premises that underlie lunar and biodynamic gardening: that plants are receptive to external forces, even celestial ones, and that aligning our gardening practices with these natural rhythms can result in healthier, more robust crops.

Dr. Rudolf Steiner

Dr. Rudolf Steiner (1861-1925) stands as one of the most intriguing and multi-dimensional figures of the 20th century. Born in Austria in 1861 and educated in Vienna, he initially made his mark in the realms of philosophy and esoteric spirituality. Yet, his intellectual pursuits were not confined to abstract thought alone; they permeated various practical disciplines, including education, medicine, and notably, agriculture. Steiner was the founder of anthroposophy and biodynamic farming—two interlinked paradigms that have had a lasting impact on our understanding of human consciousness and sustainable agriculture.

Anthroposophy, literally meaning "wisdom of the human being," is a spiritual philosophy that Steiner developed as an extension of, and a departure from, theosophy. While traditional Western thought typically separates the spiritual and physical worlds, Steiner's anthroposophy aimed to bridge that gap. It presented a holistic worldview that integrated spiritual insights with scientific understanding. Anthroposophy has not just been a subject for academic debate; it has manifested in practical endeavors, including the Waldorf education system, anthroposophical medicine, and of course, biodynamic agriculture.

Biodynamic agriculture is perhaps one of the most tangible applications of anthroposophical principles. Launched in the early 1920s, biodynamic farming emerged from a series of lectures Steiner gave, known as the "Ag-
16

riculture Course," where he introduced revolutionary ideas about farming. Steiner's approach was to view the farm as a living, self-sustaining organism that benefits from a diversified ecosystem rather than monocultural practices. His methods rejected synthetic pesticides and fertilizers, focusing instead on herbal, mineral and animal-based preparations to nourish the soil and plants.

Central to Steiner's agricultural philosophy was the notion of cosmic rhythms and their influence on plant growth. While traditional agriculture paid heed to seasons, weather and soil quality, Steiner introduced an astronomical component, citing the significance of lunar and planetary cycles. Although not the first to observe the influence of celestial bodies on terrestrial events, Steiner systematized this knowledge within the framework of biodynamics.

Steiner posited that lunar cycles, in conjunction with other planetary movements, had tangible effects on soil quality, plant growth, and animal behavior. According to his theories, different phases of the Moon and its relative position to the Earth and other planets could impact various aspects of agricultural productivity. For instance, sowing seeds when the Moon is waxing (increasing in light) could yield better germination and plant vitality, he suggested. These weren't merely astrological considerations but were rooted in the anthroposophical understanding that the cosmos and the Earth are interconnected organisms sharing life forces.

Although Steiner did not provide an exhaustive guide to lunar planting, his work laid the foundational principles upon which later researchers like Maria Thun would build. He provided enough indicators based on synodic cycles and lunar rhythms to inspire a new generation of farmers and scientists to further explore. The biodynamic farming movement, which was nascent during his time, has since burgeoned into a global community, complete with its own certification processes, educational programs, and dedicated farms that implement these celestial principles in practical agriculture.

Maria Thun and Biodynamics

Maria Thun (1922-2012) was a revered authority in the world of biodynamics, dedicating her life to studying and applying Rudolf Steiner's principles of anthroposophy and biodynamic agriculture.

Born in April 1922 near Malburg, Germany, Maria was introduced to the essence of agriculture early in her life, growing up on her father's small farm where she and her siblings actively participated in farm work. Maria's father had a unique approach to farming; he would study the evening and morning sky for several days until he intuitively sensed the right time for sowing.

Maria's journey into biodynamics began in the early 1940s when she met her future husband, Walter Thun, who introduced her to several practitioners of biodynamic farming. This encounter sparked Maria's intense interest in biodynamic methods, leading her to attend various courses at the Institute for Biodynamic Research in Darmstadt. It was here that she was introduced to Franz Rulni, a publisher of a regular planting calendar, albeit with broad and traditional advice.

Determined to understand whether the celestial constellations referred to in Rulni's calendar could aid in determining optimal sowing times, Maria initiated a series of experiments, sowing radishes and meticulously observing the variations in crops sown on different days under identical conditions.

Her work stands as a seminal chapter in the exploration of biodynamic agriculture and lunar planting methods. Though inspired by the pioneering contributions of Dr. Rudolf Steiner, Thun's research took its own distinctive trajectory. While Steiner offered a few key insights primarily based on synodic cycles, Thun set out to substantiate and expand upon these concepts through rigorous empirical study.

Maria Thun took her cue from Steiner's initial framework but delved deeper into the nuanced interplay between celestial bodies and terrestrial life. She carried out exhaustive experiments over many years, methodically observing the effects of celestial cycles on plant growth and development.

In 1956, Thun developed a procedure of sowing according to the position of the Moon in front of the twelve zodiacal constellations. These constellations were classified into four groups according to the element (Earth, Water, Air and Fire) astrologically associated with them. Root, leaf, flower and fruit crops were found to show increased yields if sown when the Moon stood before Earth, Water, Air and Fire constellations, respectively.

This wasn't a whimsical association but a theory underpinned by years of keen observation and meticulous record-keeping. She noticed that plants didn't just grow better or worse depending on the Moon's phase; different parts of the plants seemed to respond to different celestial influences.

Thun realized that when the Moon was in constellations associated with the earth element, root vegetables like carrots and beets exhibited optimal growth. Conversely, when the Moon passed through water-associated constellations, leafy greens like lettuce and spinach fared particularly well. Flowering plants seemed to thrive when the Moon was in air-related constellations, and for seed development, warmth-associated constellations were most favorable.

These observations were more than just isolated findings; they reflected an intricate cosmic dance between the heavens and the Earth. Maria Thun's work transcended mere agricultural guidelines to become a cosmological inquiry into the rhythms of the universe and their earthly echoes. It provided a systematic approach to farming that was harmoniously aligned with natural and cosmic rhythms, demonstrating that human activity could work in partnership with the broader environmental and cosmic factors.

Through her research, Thun developed her lunar planting calendar which has been updated annually and remains a key resource for biodynamic farmers and gardeners around the world. This calendar encapsulates her empirical findings, offering detailed recommendations for when to sow, transplant, and harvest different types of crops based on celestial movements. It serves as both a practical guide and a testament to her lifelong commitment to fusing ancient wisdom with empirical research.

Thun's contributions have opened up new horizons in the study of biodynamic agriculture. Researchers like Hartmut Spiess and Laurence Edwards, each in their own way, have built upon this foundation, adding further layers of understanding to the subtle interplay between terrestrial and celestial ecosystems.

Dr Hartmut Spiess:
Radish trials link celestial cycles and plant growth

Dr. Hartmut Spiess is a prominent researcher known for his work in the field of biodynamic agriculture, particularly for his extensive studies linking celestial cycles with plant growth.

In the late 1970s, he conducted an experiment focusing on radishes and how they grow in relation to the Moon's phases. This study aimed to put scientific evidence behind the age-old belief that the Moon can influence plant growth. Radishes were chosen because they have a short life cycle, making it easier to observe results.

The experiment was set up carefully. Radishes were planted at specific times to match with distinct phases of the Moon: the new Moon, first quarter, full Moon, and last quarter. Spiess made sure other variables, such as soil quality and watering, remained consistent throughout the trial. This was done to ensure that any differences in growth could be attributed to the Moon's influence and not some other factor.

After the radishes had grown to maturity, Spiess measured several aspects of their development, including the length and thickness of their roots and the overall size of the plants. The results were intriguing: radishes planted during certain lunar phases did show differences in growth compared to those planted during other phases. In particular, some Moon phases seemed to support better root development, resulting in larger and healthier radishes.

However, it's important to note that not everyone agrees with these findings. Critics argue that the observed differences in radish growth could be due to other uncontrolled factors or simply a result of statistical chance. Nonetheless, for those interested in lunar gardening—the practice of planting according to the Moon's cycles—the Spiess study offers some scientific backing.

Laurence Edwards and the interconnectedness of life on Earth and the greater universe

Lawrence Edwards (1912-2004) was a teacher of mathematics. He pursued his unique research for over thirty years, focusing on the forms of living nature in relation to geometric analysis and lectured widely all over the world. His work offers another intriguing perspective that dovetails with the exploration of lunar rhythms and plant growth. Edwards' seminal research is encapsulated in his book *"The Vortex of Life,"* published by Floris Press in 1993. His inquiry emerged from a foundational understanding of projective geometry, (a branch of mathematics that deals with geometric properties that are invariant (unchanged) under projective transformations. In simpler terms, it's concerned with the properties of figures that stay the same even when you stretch, twist, or project them onto another surface). This is a subject he explored in his earlier work published by the Rudolf Steiner Institute in 1985.

At the core of Edwards' investigation was a simple yet profound question: Does nature produce geometrically precise forms? In other words, are the natural shapes we see around us—such as buds, leaves, and eggs—created following precise geometric rules? This question is not just a matter of aesthetic curiosity; it strikes at the heart of how we understand the fundamental laws that govern life on Earth.

The findings were revealing. Mother Nature, Edwards discovered, was far from haphazard in her creative processes. Early in his research, he observed that natural forms like eggs and buds were not random but followed specific geometric principles in their structures. Contrary to any presumption of randomness or arbitrariness in nature's creations, Edwards found that these entities adhered to defined geometric principles, indicative of an underlying order and precision in the natural world.

He coined the term "path curves" to describe these specific geometric trajectories that these natural forms follow in their development or formation. The concept of "path curves" implies a predetermined route or a specific pattern in the way these forms grow or are shaped, hinting at inherent laws or guidelines that these forms seem to obey.

However, the path curves are not rigid or immutable. While they maintain the fundamental structure, their properties or parameters can exhibit variations, suggesting a dynamic aspect to the formation of these natural entities. This dynamic aspect implies adaptability and flexibility within the foundational geometry of these forms. It suggests that while there is a basic geometric framework that nature adheres to, there is also room for modification and variation within that framework, allowing for diversity in form and structure.

This variability within a structured framework highlights the simultaneous presence of order and adaptability in nature's designs. It presents a balanced interplay between consistency and variability, demonstrating how nature, in its creative processes, is both structured and versatile, capable of producing a multitude of forms that, while diverse, adhere to specific geometric principles.

As Edwards delved deeper, he made another astonishing discovery. He found a statistically significant relationship between the variation in these path curves and the relative positions of the Earth, Moon, and one other planet—which planet depended on the species being studied. The phenomenon manifested as a rhythmical elongation and relaxation of the buds, particularly evident during the winter months. In essence, these buds seemed to be engaging in a cosmic dance with celestial bodies, moving in rhythm with the heavens.

An example of this might be the buds of deciduous trees like the oak tree (*Quercus spp.*). These trees shed their leaves in the fall but retain buds throughout the winter months, which are dormant but alive. Imagine if Laurance Edwards' findings were applied to the oak tree. Throughout the winter, as most plant life lies dormant, the buds on an oak tree could be engaging in subtle but intricate rhythms influenced by the positions of the Earth, Moon, and perhaps another celestial body like Saturn or Jupiter.

As these celestial bodies align in particular formations, the oak tree's buds might experience rhythmic elongation and relaxation. It would be a dance of minuscule proportions, likely unnoticed by casual observers, but potentially of significant importance to the tree's preparation for spring. It might be a strategic way to optimize the bud's structure for the conditions it will face in the months ahead, or perhaps to maximize its potential to take advantage of light and nutrients once spring arrives.

In this way, even a sturdy, seemingly immobile oak tree could be deeply synchronized with the larger celestial ballet, its winter buds quietly preparing for the explosion of life that comes with spring, all in tune with the cosmic cycles that govern not just our planet but perhaps all life as we know it.

This work adds a layer of complexity to our understanding of plant life and its relationship with celestial cycles. Like Hartmut Spiess' lunar research, Edwards' findings invite us to look at the natural world through a lens that marries tradition, folklore and scientific investigation. The revelation that natural forms like buds exhibit rhythmic movements that correspond to the positions of celestial bodies suggests an intricate relationship between terrestrial life and the cosmos—one that we are only beginning to grasp fully.

Regenerative Farming

The term "sustainable agriculture" started gaining prominence in the 1980s as concerns about the long-term environmental impact of conventional agriculture grew. But it was around the late 1990s and early 2000s that the concept of "regenerative agriculture" began to take shape as its own distinct approach. This form of farming aims not just to sustain, but to actively improve ecological systems, focusing on soil health, water management, and ecosystem resilience, among other factors.

Notable proponents of regenerative agriculture include the Rodale Institute, a renowned research organization dedicated to pioneering organic farming through research and outreach, which has been instrumental in researching and promoting this form of farming. Other key figures include Allan Savory, who developed holistic management as a regenerative approach to livestock grazing, and permaculture co-founders Bill Mollison and David Holmgren.

The increasing awareness of climate change and its relationship with soil carbon sequestration has also given the regenerative farming movement a significant boost in the last couple of decades.

So, while the idea of working with natural systems in agriculture is ancient, the concept of "regenerative farming" as it's understood today is relatively recent, crystallizing mainly in the last 20 to 30 years.

The foundational pillar of regenerative farming is soil health, influenced by organic matter and microbial activity, which fosters a resilient ecosystem capable of resisting pests and disease. This concept can be seen as an extension of Steiner and Thun's focus on soil fertility and the importance of composting, albeit scaled to commercial applications. But what sets regenerative farming apart is its overarching goal of restoring degraded soil and ecosystems, aiming to reverse the negative impacts of traditional farming methods. Techniques like no-till farming, agroforestry, and pasture cropping come into play here, all designed to enrich the soil's organic matter and microbial life.

Another essential aspect of regenerative farming is its focus on increasing biodiversity, both above and below the soil. Diverse plant species in crop rotations and cover crops, as well as the presence of livestock, can break the pest and disease cycles, reducing the need for chemical interventions. This creates a resilient ecosystem, better equipped to adapt to changes and stresses.

Now, where does Moon gardening fit into this picture? Both regenerative farming and Moon gardening theories focus on working in harmony with natural cycles to maximize yield and improve the quality of the crop. Moon gardening pays close attention to the lunar cycles and the gravitational effects on plant growth, soil moisture, and even microbial activity. In a regenerative farming context, this can be thought of as yet another layer of fine-tuning; by aligning planting schedules with lunar cycles, farmers can take advantage of the Moon's influence to improve seed germination, optimize plant growth, and even increase the efficacy of composting practices.

Why is Moon Gardening Gaining Popularity?

Moon gardening has been gradually capturing the collective imagination of gardeners, farmers, and even urban dwellers with small terraces or window boxes. The renewed interest in this ancient practice can be attributed to a variety of factors that resonate with contemporary societal trends and concerns.

First and foremost, there's a growing awareness of the importance of sustainable and organic farming and gardening methods. As people become more educated about the environmental consequences of industrial agriculture—such as soil degradation, water pollution, and loss of biodiversity—they are increasingly seeking alternative approaches that are in harmony with natural cycles and ecosystems. Moon gardening fits perfectly into this paradigm. It promotes a deeper understanding of the natural world, encouraging gardeners to synchronize their activities with lunar phases, which can improve everything from soil quality to crop yield, without the need for synthetic fertilizers or pesticides.

Secondly, the appeal of "getting back to basics" resonates deeply with people who are overwhelmed by the fast pace and high-stress environment of modern life. Moon gardening provides an opportunity to slow down and reconnect with nature in a meaningful way. The mere act of observing the Moon's phases fosters mindfulness, instilling a sense of calm and grounding that is often missing in our digital, always-on culture.

The rise of citizen science and accessible information has also played a role. Enthusiasts can now easily access lunar calendars, read up on the specific benefits of planting or harvesting during different Moon phases and even participate in online forums where they can share tips and success stories. The democratization of information has made Moon gardening more accessible than ever before, allowing individuals to experiment, observe and come to their own conclusions about the efficacy of this practice.

Moreover, there's an intergenerational aspect to the revival of Moon gardening. Many people are rediscovering this practice through older family members, perhaps finding an old lunar calendar tucked away in a drawer, (like I did!) just as they also rediscover the importance of heirloom seeds and traditional farming techniques. This taps into a broader cultural trend that values artisanal and "authentic" experiences and fosters a sense of continuity between past and present.

In a world where ecological and personal well-being are increasingly seen as interconnected, Moon gardening offers a compelling mix of spirituality, science, and environmental stewardship. As the Moon waxes and wanes above, its gentle pull is ushering in a new era of mindful gardening below, echoing the age-old wisdom that everything is, indeed, connected.

Moon Gardening Around the World: A Tapestry of Traditions and Techniques

The allure of Moon gardening transcends national borders, weaving a rich tapestry of cultural traditions and practices worldwide. This time-honored approach to cultivation attests to humanity's long-standing fascination with the Moon and its potential influence on the Earth and its rhythms. From the terraced fields of the Himalayas to the sprawling vineyards of France, the practice of gardening by lunar phases has found unique expressions across different societies and historical contexts.

In India, the practice is often referred to as "Chandra Gardening." Here, the Moon is considered an auspicious celestial body that affects both spiritual and physical growth. Planting is generally timed with the full Moon, a phase believed to optimize fruiting and flowering. The experience is deeply spiritual: many gardeners complement their agricultural endeavors with meditation and mindfulness practices, creating a harmonious amalgam of spirituality and science.

Japan offers another compelling example with its practice of "tsukimi," or Moon viewing. This is more than just a contemplative experience; it's a spiritual occasion often tied to the harvest season. The full Moon of autumn is particularly significant, as it coincides with the harvest of rice—a staple in the Japanese diet. Thus, "tsukimi" isn't merely an aesthetic pleasure; it is closely tied to agricultural productivity, emphasizing the Moon's importance in the natural cycles that sustain life.

The Philippines embraces lunar-based agricultural practices as well, scheduling planting and harvesting around the Moon's phases. During the waxing Moon, as the Moon's light grows, planting takes place to capitalize on its increasing gravitational pull. Conversely, the waning Moon—marked by its diminishing size—signals the ideal time for harvesting.

In Ancient Greece, the Moon's influence in agriculture was documented by none other than Aristotle. He posited that the Moon's gravitational force had an effect on soil moisture, making certain phases more conducive for planting than others. His ideas, embedded in scrolls and parchments, echo in modern-day agricultural science, lending an air of antiquity to contemporary practices.

In the Americas, indigenous cultures from the Navajo in the Southwest to the Mapuche in Southern Chile have long followed lunar patterns for their agricultural activities. For these cultures, the lunar calendar is a vital aspect of their worldview, a guide for both spiritual and physical sustenance.

Aotearoa New Zealand brings us the Maramataka, or Māori lunar gardening. This comprehensive system, grounded in Māori traditions, combines lunar phases with star positions and local weather patterns. The Maramata-ka has become increasingly popular today as both a repository of ancient wisdom and a guide for sustainable agriculture. It embodies a holistic view of environmental stewardship, seamlessly integrating the spiritual and the practical.

In fact, indigenous practices like Māori lunar gardening are enjoying a revival, as a new generation looks to glean wisdom from ancestral knowledge systems. This interest is part of a broader global trend that recognizes the importance of indigenous wisdom in promoting sustainable practices and addressing contemporary environmental challenges.

Gardeners and researchers globally are now probing the secrets of lunar cycles, conducting studies to quantify their impact on plant growth. As we stand on the threshold of this exciting new epoch, the surge in interest in Moon gardening offers a beautiful blend of the old and the new. It creates an enriching confluence of ancient practices and modern science, giving us a plethora of options to cultivate gardens that are not just productive but are in true harmony with the celestial and terrestrial worlds.

Biodynamic Gardening , Moon Gardening and Organics

Biodynamic Gardening, Moon Gardening, and Organic Gardening are interconnected philosophies, each grounded in a profound respect for nature and its rhythms. Each practice, while related, has its unique methodologies, philosophies, and scope. This book aims to explain these differences and offer insights into how each approach can harmonize and enrich your garden ecosystem.

Biodynamic Gardening: A Unified Ecosystem
Biodynamic gardening, stemming from Dr. Rudolf Steiner's teachings, perceives the garden as a singular living entity, a reflection of the larger cosmos. This approach sees every component—soil, plant, and cosmic rhythm—as interconnected, forming a cohesive whole.

Practitioners employ specialized techniques, applying specially-prepared compost, herbal and mineral treatments in accordance with lunar and astrological cycles to harmonize the garden with terrestrial and celestial energies. Beyond mere planting or harvesting, biodynamic gardening embraces ethical and ecological considerations, aspiring to cultivate self-sustaining ecosystems that enrich both the garden and the wider environment.

Moon Gardening: Focused and Aligned

Moon gardening, conversely, concentrates on aligning gardening tasks with lunar cycles. It recognizes the Moon's influence on plant growth but doesn't envelop the wider philosophic or ethical dimensions of biodynamic gardening. It is an accessible approach, offering those new to celestial gardening a less intensive entry point, while still allowing for deeper engagement with the garden's ecosystem.

Organic Gardening: A Holistic Approach

Organic gardening emphasizes sustainability, biodiversity, and the avoidance of synthetic chemicals and GMOs. It prioritizes soil health, utilizing natural fertilizers and ecological pest control, and champions the use of non-GMO and heirloom seeds, thus promoting a harmonious and balanced garden environment. Moon gardening can be considered a specialized form of organic gardening, providing a unique perspective to manage and understand your garden's needs.

Inside the Book

This book explores the intricacies of moon, biodynamic and organic gardening practices. While my own practice is deeply rooted in organic gardening, enriched with lunar influences, the insights and advice from diverse biodynamic gardening practitioners offer a well-rounded exploration of biodynamic gardening philosophies.

The discussions will often lean towards strategies to enhance your organic gardening experience, with a focus on aligning these strategies with lunar phases for optimal results, inviting you to a deeper, more connected way of gardening.

Welcome to a world where the celestial and the terrestrial dance in harmony—welcome to the world of Moon gardening.

CHAPTER 2.

Beginners Guide to Moon Gardening

Now that we've covered the basics behind lunar gardening, it's time to get our hands dirty. But before diving into the nuts and bolts of orienting your garden to the lunar calendar, let's look at how the Moon affects your growing space. Understanding these lunar phases and their respective impacts enables Moon gardeners to make well-informed decisions on when to plant, maintain, and harvest their crops.

Understanding the Lunar Cycle
The Moon orbits Earth in approximately 27.3 days, a period known as a sidereal month. However, because Earth is also revolving around the sun, the phases of the Moon as observed from Earth unfold over a slightly longer lunar month of about 29.5 days. Throughout this month, the Moon transitions through four primary phases: the New Moon, First Quarter, Full Moon, and Third Quarter.

The lunar cycle can be divided into two main segments: the waxing phase and the waning phase. During the waxing phase, which spans from the New Moon to the Full Moon, the Moon's illumination increases. Conversely, in the waning phase, the Moon's light diminishes as it transitions from the Full Moon back to a New Moon.

By aligning your gardening activities with these lunar phases, you can leverage the natural rhythms of plant growth to your advantage. Each phase offers its own set of optimal conditions for specific gardening tasks and we'll explore these in the chapters that follow.

Monthly Lunar Cycle Checklists
New Moon Phase (New Moon to First Quarter)

This is a time of rising vitality in your garden.
The tasks you complete should focus on preparing your space for growth.

The New Moon phase, stretching from the New Moon to the First Quarter, marks a time of burgeoning vitality in your garden. During this period, lunar gravity exerts its pull, drawing water up through the soil and invigorating your plants. The incrementally increasing Moonlight also spurs leaf growth. This is the perfect time to concentrate on setting the stage for a flourishing garden. Below is an expanded checklist to help you capitalize on this auspicious period.

New Moon Phase To-Do Checklist

Weed Your Garden Beds: Eliminate weeds that could steal valuable nutrients and water from your plants. This prevents future competition and helps your garden focus its energy on growth.

Prepare Your Garden Beds: Remove any old plant material and break up clods of earth to create a fine tilth. This prepares your beds for the planting that follows.

Soil Cultivation: Loosen the soil with a garden fork or a hoe to a depth of at least 6 to 8 inches, enhancing its aeration and water absorption capabilities.

Apply Organic Fertilizers: Enrich your garden soil with organic matter like compost, bone meal, or well-rotted manure. This not only adds nutrients but also improves soil structure.

Install Support Structures: If you're growing climbing plants like tomatoes, peas, or cucumbers, set up trellises or stakes to support their upward growth.

Plant Above-Ground Crops: This is an excellent time to sow seeds for plants that grow above the ground, such as lettuce, spinach, and various herbs. If you prefer, you can also delay this task until the First Quarter phase for better Moonlight exposure.

Pruning: Remove dead, diseased, or damaged branches from trees and shrubs to encourage new growth and better air circulation. Always use clean, sharp tools to make clean cuts.

Initiate or Supplement a Compost Pile: If you don't already have a compost pile, now's a great time to start one. If you do have one, consider adding green and brown materials to kickstart the decomposition process.

Tend to Miscellaneous Tasks: Utilize this time to complete any odd jobs around the garden. This might include repairing fences, cleaning tools, or installing new garden beds.

By aligning your activities with the New Moon phase, you'll be working in harmony with natural forces that encourage growth and vitality. The idea is not just to do tasks for the sake of doing them, but to perform them at a time when they will be most effective.

First Quarter Phase (First Quarter to Full Moon)

*This is the most prolific time for sowing and planting
all the produce above the ground.*

The first quarter phase of the lunar cycle is a period of increasing vitality and growth, especially for plants that bear their crops above ground. At this time, the intensifying Moonlight provides a potent source of energy that encourages leaf growth. Plants like tomatoes, beans, and broccoli flourish when sown or transplanted during this phase. Conversely, it's best to hold off on planting root crops, as the focus on above-ground leafy growth can inhibit proper root development.

During the 48 hours leading up to the full Moon, be prepared for rapid germination. However, this burst of energy may lead to frail, spindly plants that are vulnerable to damping off, pests, and diseases.

First Quarter Phase To-Do Checklist:

Optimal Watering: The waxing Moon, including this first quarter phase, is believed to enhance water uptake in plants. It's an ideal time to water, as the lunar energy works in tandem with plants to promote growth.

Division and Transplantation: Well-established plants, especially perennials and some shrubs, can be divided and transplanted to other parts of your garden. This task is particularly effective during this phase, when plant energy is directed towards new growth.

Successful Propagation: If you're interested in propagating new plants, taking cuttings during the first quarter phase is advisable. The strong lunar influence promotes quicker rooting and more vigorous growth.

Grafting Young Trees: This is an opportune period for grafting. The sap flows more freely, aiding the healing process and facilitating better graft union.

Boost Soil Health: Don't let your soil go neglected. Infuse it with compost, organic matter and other essential nutrients. As the full Moon approaches, it's an excellent time to apply liquid manure to maximize nutrient absorption.

Planting and Transplanting Above-Ground Crops: Use this lunar phase to your advantage by continuing to plant or transplant fruiting annuals. Think tomatoes, beans, peas, cauliflower, pumpkin and broccoli. These plants thrive in the conditions fostered by the increasing moonlight.

Caution with Root Crops: Avoid planting carrots, potatoes and other root crops. Rapid leaf growth at this time can be at the expense of root development. Also, these plants may bolt, or go to seed, more quickly than desired.

Pest and Disease Watch: Be vigilant. Monitor your garden closely for signs of pests and diseases and act swiftly to mitigate any issues. Slugs and snails, in particular, tend to be more active during this period.

Initiate Composting: If you haven't started a compost pile yet, now is the time. The lunar energy during this phase accelerates the decomposition process, turning your kitchen scraps and yard waste into valuable soil nutrients faster.

A Note on Pruning: Pruning is discouraged during this time. The high sap flow can lead to excessive bleeding of cut branches and potential dieback. By following these guidelines in tune with the first quarter of the lunar cycle, you're setting the stage for a garden that not only survives but thrives, in harmony with the celestial rhythms.

Full Moon Phase (Full Moon to Third Quarter)

The full Moon is the period of maximum light,
and it's a time of fast growth.
Plants will germinate quickly during this time.

The full Moon is a luminary peak in the lunar cycle, casting maximum light on your garden. It's an important time for root development and fast growth, thanks to the strong gravitational pull that keeps soil well-moisturized. The full Moon to the third quarter is particularly auspicious for planting root crops and perennial plants that require a more extended period for root development. Moreover, this is the time when your garden will benefit from important maintenance activities such as weeding, pruning, and disease control.

Full Moon Phase To-Do Checklist:

Fruiting Perennials and Flowers: This is a fortuitous phase for planting fruiting perennials and flowering plants, including apple trees, asparagus, and rhubarb. The full Moon's energy supports their long-term growth.

Lawn Care: Consider sowing grass seed over your lawn during this phase. The moisture-retentive soil offers the perfect environment for quick germination and root development.

Plant Root Crops: As the third quarter nears, it's the optimal time for planting all manner of root vegetables—carrots, beets, onions, potatoes, and garlic. These plants will benefit from the moisture-rich soil.

Weed Management: Weeds are also enjoying a growth spurt at this time. Keep your garden tidy by hand-pulling weeds or applying an organic weed killer. The efficacy of weed control sprays is particularly high during this period.

Pest and Disease Control: Continue to monitor your plants for signs of pests and diseases. Due to the high soil moisture content, disease propagation is more likely. Opt for sprays that can work effectively in this high-moisture environment.

Deadheading and Leaf Maintenance: Remove spent flowers and dead leaves to enhance plant health and aesthetics. This simple task prevents potential diseases and focuses the plant's energy on new growth.

Pruning Post-Bloom: For plants that have finished their blooming cycle, now is a great time to prune. The pruning will help maintain their shape and encourage new growth, making them even more beautiful in the next season.

General Garden Improvement: Utilize this period to add mulch, build or repair fences, and carry out other general garden improvements. These activities will prepare your garden for the different phases of growth and dormancy throughout the year.

Final Quarter Phase (Third Quarter to New Moon)

This final quarter phase in the lunar cycle is your garden's seasonal "down-time," an opportunity to harvest, maintain, and plan.

As the Moon wanes toward the new Moon, you enter a period of slow growth and harvest. The lesser Moonlight and weaker gravitational pull create conditions that favor soil improvement and maintenance over planting. This final quarter phase is a time for reaping what you've sown, refining your garden space, and focusing on activities that fortify the health of your plants for future cycles.

Final Quarter Phase To-Do Checklist:

Harvest Time: Harvest all crops that are mature and ready for picking. This is the prime time to reap the fruits, vegetables, and herbs you've been cultivating.

Weed Control and Garden Cleanup: The slow growth phase is ideal for weed removal. Take the opportunity to remove any invasive weeds, dead foliage, and diseased plant material. Cultivating the soil at this time can help prevent future weed growth.

Lawn Maintenance: Use this period to mow your lawn, ensuring that the weaker gravitational pull minimizes stress on the grass. This will contribute to a lush, even lawn in the growing seasons ahead.

Pruning Activities: With sap levels at their lowest, this is the best time to prune trees and shrubs. This will redirect the plant's energy toward root development, fortifying its resilience for future growing cycles.

Soil Enrichment: Given that this is a less active phase for planting, focus on improving the soil. Add layers of mulch and compost to retain moisture and enrich the soil. If you haven't already, consider soil testing to determine what nutrients may be lacking.

Transplanting and Fertilizing: If you need to transplant any perennials, now is the time. The low sap run and weak gravitational pull reduce plant stress, making transplantation more successful. Apply fertilizers that target root growth to support your plants for the next growth cycle.

Focus on Below-Ground Activities: Since this is a period where the energy is being pulled back into the earth, consider activities that focus on root zone health, such as aerating the soil.

Garden Assessment: Use this quieter period to take stock of your garden. Note what worked well and what didn't, and plan for the next lunar cycle. This is also an excellent time to clean, sharpen, and repair your garden tools, ensuring you're well-prepared for the next planting season.

The Weather and You

Beyond synchronizing your garden tasks with the Moon's phases, it is important to remember that there are two other things that influence your garden—the weather and you!

If the weather is wrong for the task you have scheduled, that should take precedence over what the Moon phase might be and if the timing is wrong for you, then don't stress it—stressed out gardeners are no good for the garden.

If you've got time and patience enough to pay close attention to what's going on in your garden, your garden will be able to tell you what it needs. In daily practice, the weather, soil conditions, lateness of season and so on often overrides considerations of a cosmic nature!

How to Use a Moon Calendar for Gardeners

One of the best ways to take the guesswork out of what task to do in which quarter of the Moon's phases is by using a portable Moon calendar. The Moon Calendar by Supernature Stores is a perpetual calendar that's designed for ease of use. It focuses on the changing Moon phases to show you the dates best suited for germination, spraying, pruning, feeding the soil, light cultivation, sowing seeds, and even when to look for garden pests like slugs and snails.

This calendar is made with two wheels hinged on a central rivet that spin independently. Simply turn the inner wheel to correspond with the date of the new Moon phase for each month and follow the calendar's instructions as the days progress. This is a perpetual calendar, meaning this same calendar can be used indefinitely, no matter where you live, year after year.

With this single, enduring tool, you can simplify your lunar gardening for the long term.

Shop on Amazon: www.amazon.com/dp/B07W3R372Z

Work with the Seasons

It may seem obvious, but just to be clear, you need to be working with the seasons, not simply the monthly lunar phases when prescribing garden tasks. To illustrate the point, imagine you're a conductor preparing to lead an orchestra through Vivaldi's "Four Seasons." You have all the sheet music aligned, your baton is poised, and the musicians are at the ready. However, you suddenly decide to mix movements from "Spring" into "Winter." It might still be beautiful, but it's not what Vivaldi intended, and the audience will feel the discord.

In the same way, Moon gardening isn't just about following lunar cycles; it's about syncing these cycles with the natural rhythms of the Earth's seasons. You wouldn't sow your tomatoes in the dead of winter just because it's a New Moon, right? Each season is like a different movement in a symphony, each with its own tempo, melody, and range of instruments—or in gardening terms, its own set of suitable crops and garden tasks.

The lunar calendar can guide you on when to do something, but the Earth's seasons tell you what is appropriate to do. It's like the difference between knowing the right timing to pluck a violin string (Moon cycle) and knowing which musical note it should be (season). Both need to be in harmony for the garden—your earthy orchestra—to truly flourish.

So, as you plot out your garden tasks by the lunar phases, remember to layer those insights atop the wisdom of the changing seasons. It's not just about doing the right thing; it's about doing the right thing at the right time, in the right season.

CHAPTER 3:

Diving Deeper into Lunar and Biodynamic Gardening

Gardening by the lunar cycle offers a multitude of approaches, each with its unique blend of tradition, science, and folklore. In the previous chapter, we introduced you to the Moon Calendar for Gardeners, a tool that simplifies lunar gardening by focusing solely on the Moon's phases. It's a straightforward method that may perfectly suit your lifestyle and level of desired complexity.

Yet, the art of gardening is as varied as the gardeners themselves. How you approach your garden is a reflection not only of the celestial patterns above but also of your own unique blend of intuition, skill, and observation. After all, gardening is a dialogue between you and the Earth, one where your voice is as influential as the Moon's cycles and the zodiac's whispers.

The Biodynamic Perspective: Uniting Earth and Cosmos
Many practitioners of biodynamic gardening have shared with me their profound sense of interconnectedness between our planet and the cosmos. This is more than just a feeling; it's a guiding philosophy that animates their gardening practices, bringing a vibrant, life-affirming energy to their gardens.

Biodynamic Lunar Gardening Principles

If you're willing to explore beyond the Moon phases to prescribe garden tasks as described in the last chapter, the Biodynamic gardening calendar might offer a more intricate, nuanced methodology. Unlike the simpler Moon Gardener's Calendar, which is a perpetual guide, the biodynamic calendar is released yearly and marries astrological wisdom with agricultural best practices. This approach was masterfully devised by Maria Thun and has garnered a loyal following.

The biodynamic calendar extends the principles of lunar gardening well past the Moon's phases. It factors in the Moon's ascending or descending path across the sky and even considers the zodiac constellations the Moon travels in front of during its lunar journey. But it doesn't stop there. The biodynamic approach also takes into account what part of the plant—be it root, leaf, flower, or fruit—requires attention or stimulation at any given time.

To follow Biodynamic gardening practice you will need to use a biodynamic calendar. Maria Thun's annual Biodynamic gardening calendar is available online or contact your local Biodyanimc Assocation to get one of theirs. To follow explains the moon's path, the stars and constellations as they relate to biodynamic gardening methods.

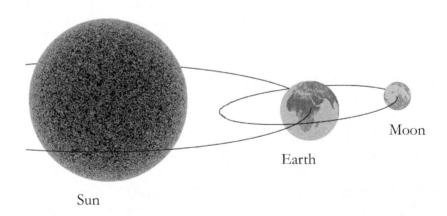

Sun

Earth

Moon

The Moon's journey across the sky, as viewed from Earth, is a mesmerizing dance of celestial mechanics, a performance that never exactly repeats. While we may observe it rising and setting, the Moon also follows a vertical path, tracing a route that is sometimes higher in the sky, and at other times, lower. This vertical motion is often categorized into two phases: ascending and descending.

As it turns out, the Moon completes its zodiacal circle in about 27.3 days, known as a sidereal month. Within this cycle, the Moon spends roughly two weeks in its ascending phase and another two weeks in its descending phase. Fascinatingly, the Moon accomplishes in one month what the sun takes an entire year to do.

Geography also plays a role in this celestial ballet. Near the poles, the Moon's vertical path is more pronounced, while closer to the equator, its influence appears subtler. The Moon's gravitational impact on plants, for instance, is diluted at the equator, underscoring the geographically nuanced interplay between lunar cycles and terrestrial life.

In the realm of astronomy, a sidereal month serves as a precise temporal yardstick to gauge the Moon's orbit around Earth in relation to the fixed stars. While a sidereal month spans approximately 27.3 days, it's crucial to differentiate it from the synodic month, which lasts around 29.5 days. The synodic month measures the time it takes for the Moon to complete its full phase cycle, from new Moon back to new Moon. The slight discrepancy in duration arises from Earth's own journey around the sun, which subtly shifts the Moon's relative position to us and extends the synodic cycle.

The sidereal month's significance extends beyond mere lunar tracking. It acts as a celestial reference frame that assists astronomers in precisely determining the Moon's position relative to other cosmic entities. This knowledge is indispensable for celestial observations, navigations, and calculations that involve not only our Moon but the entire heavenly tableau.

An intriguing geographical corollary to consider is that when the Moon is ascending in the Northern Hemisphere, it's descending in the Southern Hemisphere, much like the inverse relationship between summer in one hemisphere and winter in the other. This beautiful symmetry reveals the complex, interconnected dance between Earth and Moon—a ballet that influences not just tides and seasons but also the subtle rhythms of life on our planet.

The Ascending Moon—Nature's Uplifting Phase

In the cosmic rhythm, the ascending phase of the Moon resonates like the hopeful seasons of spring and summer on Earth. It's a time when nature seems to inhale deeply, filling its lungs with life-giving energy. During this period, the Moon embarks on an upward trajectory in the sky, starting low and gradually reaching toward its zenith—the highest point it will touch in this cycle. Over roughly two weeks, the Moon not only ascends but also lingers longer in the night sky.

This upward movement has a tangible impact on Earth, especially in the plant kingdom. Picture the sap in plants as responding to an upward call, making it an especially favorable period for grafting or harvesting crops that grow above the ground.

When the Earth 'exhales' during this ascending phase, conditions become favorable for sowing seeds. The energies at play here don't just boost your spirits; they invigorate the seeds, nudging them into the first stages of life. The ascending Moon's energy is like nature's growth serum, making it an optimal period for planting new seeds and initiating the growth cycles of various crops.

So, as you plan your gardening tasks, keep an eye on the Moon's path. When it's ascending, you're not just witnessing a celestial event; you're given a cue by nature herself. This is the time to sow, to plant, to reach for the sky—just like the Moon.

When we see the arch of the Moon path getting higher in the sky every day, the Moon is ascending.

The Descending Moon—The Earth's Restful Exhale

In contrast to the ascending Moon's energetic expansion, the descending path ushers in a more contemplative mood, echoing the earth's inward-turning energy during autumn and winter. Over approximately two weeks, the Moon starts at its zenith and follows a descending trajectory, each night sinking lower and lower in the sky until it hugs the horizon, as if gently laying itself to rest.

This celestial descent has implications for your garden, signaling a shift towards contraction and conservation of energy. It's as if the earth takes a deep, grounding breath in, calling the sap in plants to flow downward. This makes it an advantageous time for tasks that require strong root development, like transplanting or preparing the soil for future growth.

As the sap descends, roots find a renewed intimacy with the soil, optimizing conditions for root expansion and fortifying plant health. During this phase, the Moon effectively whispers to the earth, instructing it to focus on establishing strong, deep roots.

The ebb and flow of the Moon's ascending and descending phases offer a roadmap for your gardening journey. To maximize your efforts, align your gardening activities with these lunar rhythms. Sow and plant under the ascending Moon, taking advantage of the earth's energetic exhale. Conversely, use the descending Moon's inward focus to transplant and fortify the soil, setting the stage for long-term plant health and stability.

Understanding this celestial choreography enables you to garden in harmony with the earth's natural rhythms.

When we see the arc of the Moon path getting lower every day, the Moon is descending

A Moon Gardener Shares her Lunar Experience (name withheld)

"When I first dipped my toes into Moon gardening, I kept it simple. Ascending Moon meant it was time to sow seeds. Descending Moon? Perfect for transplanting. It was a rhythm that clicked for me, easy to remember and easy to follow.

Years back, I was also working part-time at a hydroponic farm. There, the schedule was set: sow seeds on Monday, wash pots on Tuesday, and harvest Wednesday through Friday. But something was off. I was standing with my boss in the spinach house one day, and he says, "Everything's perfect—water, nutrients, you name it. So why the inconsistent growth?"

That's when I told him, "It's to do with the Moon." He already thought I was a bit out there, so this just confirmed it for him. But I took my Moon calendar the next day and laid out the data. Sure enough, you could see the waves of different plant heights and growth rates depending on whether we'd sown during an ascending or descending Moon path.

That was my "aha" moment. Seeing the visible difference in plant growth was like my own personal control test. I thought, "Holy cow, this Moon thing really works!"

I've been at this for six years now, and I can't imagine gardening any other way. The structure it gives me, the pest resistance, the higher yields—I wouldn't trade it for anything. It's more than a gardening strategy; it's a lifestyle."

The Moon and Stars and Constellations

In biodynamic gardening, the influence of the Moon and constellations plays a significant role in the planting and cultivation process. While the belt of stars and constellations remains fixed in the sky, the Moon and planets move in front of this celestial backdrop on their own orbits.

As the Moon progresses through each constellation over the course of a month, it brings the specific influence of that sign to the Earth during various gardening activities like sowing, planting, cultivating and harvesting.

Root days, leaf days, flower days, and fruit days

B iodynamic calendars utilize the concept of root days, leaf days, flower days, and fruit days, which correspond to the passage of the Moon in front of the different constellations. These designations are represented by colors and zodiac signs on the calendar. It's important to note that the lunar cycle consists of 12 unequal sectors derived from the stellar constellations, which may differ from the traditional astrological division of equal 30-degree sections.

Each constellation is associated with one of the four elements: **Air, Water, Fire,** and **Earth**. These elements correspond to specific aspects of plant growth and development.

 EARTH is linked to the mineral element and root crops like carrots. (Root days)

 WATER is associated with leaves and photosynthesis. (Leaf days)

 AIR is connected with flowers, bees, pollen and fragrance. (Flower days)

 FIRE is connected to the ripening of sweet fruit and the warmth of the sun. (Fruit/seed days)

◊ **Each sign corresponds to an element which in turn corresponds to the best crops to plant.**

Astrological "best days" in biodynamic gardening take into account the Moon's position in the sidereal astrological zodiac. Throughout the course of a month, the Moon passes in front of each sign of the zodiac, spending approximately 2.5 days in each sign. The constellations also are different sizes. For instance, the Moon only spends half a day in Libra, but three and a half days in Virgo. This research comes from Maria Thun, who observed that the constellation Moon relationship has an effect on a particular part

45

of the plant rather than the whole plant. She determined the zodiac sign corresponds to an element, and these elements are associated with the best crops to plant during those particular periods.

When the Moon is in front of a particular constellation, it stimulates the corresponding element of the plant. This understanding is important because different parts or aspects of a plant require nurturing based on their purpose. For example, when growing tomato plants, the emphasis is on cultivating their fruits rather than their leaves, roots, or flowers. Similarly, carrots are grown for their roots, spinach for its leaves, and lavender for its flowers.

It's worth noting that many vegetables that grow above the ground, such as tomatoes, cucumbers, beans, and peas, are classified as fruits in the context of biodynamics. This classification extends beyond what we traditionally perceive as fruits, encompassing strawberries, apples, pears, plums, cherries and more.

There is also a relationship between the different types of days. Root and leaf days complement each other, as do flower and fruit/seed days. For example, the second-best day for planting root crops would be a leaf day, while for fruit-bearing plants, a flower day is considered favorable. Additionally, most plants can benefit from planting on a root day since all plants have roots that require strong development.

Celestial signs or astrological signs?
In biodynamic gardening, celestial signs are indeed closely related to astrological signs, as both are derived from the position and movement of celestial bodies, particularly the Moon, in the zodiac.

In addition to the zodiac, the lunar phases are paramount in biodynamic practices. Specific gardening tasks like sowing, pruning, harvesting are timed according to the waxing and waning of the Moon, and its position in the zodiac.

Practitioners of biodyanimcs believe the correlation of celestial and astrological signs reflects a holistic approach to agriculture, where cosmic rhythms and terrestrial processes are seen as interconnected components of a unified whole.

Earth Constellations

Root days: The Moon passes one of the earth constellations:
Capricorn,
Taurus,
Virgo

Root days:

Root days in biodynamic gardening are specific periods when the Moon passes through one of the earth constellations, namely Capricorn, Taurus, and Virgo. These days are particularly favorable for cultivating root crops such as potatoes, sweet potatoes, carrots, parsnips, onions, garlic, and radishes. The energy of the earth element enhances the growth and development of roots, providing a solid foundation for these underground crops.

Plant: When planting root crops, it is recommended to do so during the descending lunar orbit. This means choosing a time when the Moon is moving from its highest point in the sky to the horizon. Planting during this path allows the energy of the Moon to draw the sap of the plants downward, promoting strong root development.

Sow: Sowing seeds for root crops is best done on root days, preferably when the Moon is waning. The waning phase occurs after the full Moon when the illuminated portion of the Moon gradually decreases. This phase is associated with the energy of contraction and is believed to be conducive to root growth.

Fertilize: Fertilization should also be timed during a waning Moon. The decreased illumination during this phase is believed to enhance the absorption of nutrients by the plants' roots. Applying fertilizers during this time ensures that the plants can efficiently utilize the nutrients for their growth and development.

Harvest: When it comes to harvesting and storing root crops, it is ideal to do so on root days when the Moon is descending. Since root crops grow below the ground, harvesting them during this phase aligns with their natural cycle and enhances their quality and storage potential.

Water Constellations ▽

Leaf days: The Moon passes one of the water constellations:

Pisces,
Scorpio,
Cancer

Leaf days:

W ater signs, which encompass Cancer, Scorpio, and Pisces, are associated with the element of Water in astrology. These periods offer favorable conditions for cultivating leafy crops such as spinach, lettuce, and various leafy greens. The water element present during these days nurtures the lush growth of leaves and facilitates the essential process of photosynthesis.

Planting or Pruning: Engage in planting or pruning tasks, including hedges, during the descending Moon phase. This is the period when the sap is drawn down to the roots. By synchronizing your activities with the descending Moon, you promote healthy root development.

Sowing Seeds: When it comes to sowing leafy plants like spinach, lettuce, and other leafy greens, opt for leaf days that align with a waxing Moon phase. The increasing lunar energy during this time supports the germination and growth of leafy crops.

Fertilization: Timing your fertilization activities during a waning Moon phase is recommended. The waning Moon corresponds to a period when the soil is inhaling, making it more receptive to nutrient absorption. Ideally, choose a leaf day for fertilizing, as it complements the leafy growth associated with water signs.

Harvesting: Harvesting is generally best when the Moon is ascending. However, when it comes to storing your leaf harvest, it is advisable to use fruit or flower days instead. The water element present on leaf days is NOT ideal for long-term storage. By utilizing fruit or flower days for storing, you can maintain the quality and freshness of your harvested leafy crops.

Air Constellations

Flower days: The Moon passes one of the air constellations:
Gemini
Libra
Aquarius

Flower days

Air signs, which include Gemini, Libra, and Aquarius, are associated with the element of Air in astrology. These periods are particularly favorable for cultivating flowering plants and crops, such as cauliflower, broccoli, and various types of flowers. Additionally, these days are well-suited for tending to flowering herbs like chamomile, flowering hedges, and flowering trees like lilac. The air element present during these times fosters crucial processes such as pollination, resulting in vibrant blooms and the production of healthy flowers.

Plant and Prune: Engage in planting and pruning tasks when the Moon is in its descending phase. Ideally, choose flower days for these activities, as the downward movement of the Moon's energy draws sap towards the roots, promoting strong root development.

Sowing Seeds: When it comes to sowing seeds, (flower vegetables such as cauliflower and broccoli, as well as flowers) prefer flower days coinciding with a waxing Moon phase. The increasing lunar energy during this period is believed to support the germination and growth of plants.

Fertilization: Take advantage of the waning Moon phase for fertilizing your plants. During this time, the soil has better capacity to absorb nutrients. Applying fertilizers while the Moon is decreasing in illumination can enhance nutrient uptake by the plants.

Grafting, Storing, and Harvesting: For grafting activities, storing bulbs, or harvesting flowering herbs, aim for flower days when the Moon is ascending. During this phase, the upward movement of the Moon's energy corresponds to the rising sap within plants, which can aid in successful grafting, efficient bulb storage, and optimal harvests of flowering herbs. Picking flowers on flower days, preferably also before noon, will help them to remain fresher and keep their colour for longer.

Fire Constellations

Fruit days: The Moon passes one of the water constellations:
Aires
Sagittarius
Leo

Fruit days

Fruit days, associated with the Fire signs Aries, Leo, and Sagittarius, are particularly beneficial for cultivating fruit-bearing plants and crops. This includes a wide range of fruits such as strawberries, raspberries, apples, plums, as well as fruiting vegetables like tomatoes, zucchini, peppers, and beans. The fire element present during these days promotes the ripening of fruits and the development of seeds.

Planting or Replanting Seedlings: Engage in planting or replanting seedlings, especially fruit trees, during the descending Moon phase. This is when the sap is drawn down to the roots, supporting the establishment and growth of the plant.

Sowing Seeds: When it comes to fruiting vegetables, such as tomatoes, cucumbers, and others, choose fruit days that align with a waxing Moon phase for sowing the seeds. The increasing lunar energy during this period enhances the germination and growth of these plants.

Fertilization: Timing your fertilization activities during a waning Moon phase is recommended. The waning Moon corresponds to a period when the soil is inhaling and actively absorbing nutrients. Ideally, choose fruit days for fertilizing fruit plants and vegetables, as it aligns with their specific growth characteristics.

Harvesting and Grafting: Harvesting fruits and fruiting vegetables, as well as grafting fruit trees and shrubs, is best done during an ascending Moon phase. This is when the sap is rising within the plant, promoting optimal flavor and quality. Aim to perform these tasks on fruit days to harness the beneficial energy associated with the fire element.

In Summary

Planting, transplanting, and pruning
When it comes to planting, transplanting, and pruning, it's best to do so during the Moon's descending path. Keep an eye out for favorable root, flower, leaf, and fruit days to optimize your efforts.

Cutting Grass: The same logic applies as pruning – the best time is therefore on a descending Moon preferably on a leaf day.

Harvesting, Storing, and Grafting: For harvesting, storing, and grafting, choose the Moon's ascending path. However, if you're storing non-root crops, it's better to avoid leaf days to ensure better preservation.

Fertilizing, Watering: When it comes to fertilizing, watering, or applying anything that needs to be absorbed by the soil, aim to do so during the waning Moon phase. This is when the soil is more receptive to these substances.

Sowing Seeds: If you're sowing seeds for plants above the ground, try to do it during the waxing Moon. Look for relevant days based on whether it's a leaf, fruit, or flower crop. But if you're sowing root crops, it's better to do so during the waning Moon.

Trust your Intuition
Finding time for gardening can be a challenge, especially when it needs to fit around your other commitments. If you're unable to pick and choose the optimal day, don't worry! Simply try to align with the Moon phase and path as much as possible. Even small adjustments can make a difference in your gardening endeavors.

But here's the thing: you don't have to follow this approach blindly. Gardening is a dynamic and personal experience, and sometimes the best day to get your hands dirty is simply the day you have available. Trust your intuition and tap into the wisdom that already resides within you and the nature around you. By observing and listening to cues from yourself and your environment, you'll develop a more intuitive approach to gardening.

The Moon Opposite Saturn Cycle:
A Cosmic Dance of Growth and Resilience

In the holistic practice of biodynamic gardening, the celestial move-
ments hold significant sway over your gardening activities. One such crucial
astral event is when the Moon is in opposition to Saturn—a cycle that
occurs approximately every 27.5 days.

Cosmic Influences on Plant Growth
When the Moon and Saturn align opposite each other in the celestial sphere,
relative to the Earth, their unique gravitational and magnetic forces interact
in a way that influences various biological processes on our planet. Each
celestial body contributes specific qualities to plant growth:

◊ Moon's Influence: Lunar forces are said to engage
with calcium processes in plants, encouraging propagation, germination, and the development of growth
forms.

◊ Saturn's Influence: Saturn's forces are associated with
silica processes that strengthen the structural components of plants, fortifying roots, leaves, and fruits.

A Balance of Forces for Robust Plants
During the Moon opposite Saturn phase, these seemingly disparate forces
harmonize to create a balanced, nurturing environment on Earth. This cosmic alignment is thought to provide an optimal window for sowing seeds
and transplanting seedlings. Plants cultivated during this period are believed
to benefit from an interplay of lunar and Saturnian forces, which bolsters
their strength and resilience.

Enhanced Resistance to Common Garden Ailments
Biodynamic gardeners have observed that seeds sown or seedlings transplanted during this specific phase seem to exhibit heightened resistance to
common garden afflictions. Plants are more robust against fungal diseases
like powdery mildew and tomato blight. Furthermore, their natural defens-
es against insect attacks also appear to be enhanced.

A Recurring Cosmic Opportunity

Since the Moon Opposite Saturn alignment happens every 27.5 days, it's a predictable event that gardeners can anticipate and plan for. This cyclical pattern allows one to align gardening activities with cosmic rhythms, offering a recurring opportunity to work in harmony with the broader universe.

For practitioners of biodynamic gardening, this isn't just a day in the lunar calendar; it's the day you absolutely should be in the garden, sowing, planting, and nurturing.

A Moon Gardener

Shares her Experience:

"I can tell a whole year out by using the Biodynamic calendar this important day which I always need to be on the farm. As we grow so many different varieties on our property, this is a good general planting day, it helps everything.

So I can sow my broccoli, I can sow my cut flowers, I can sow tomatoes, I can sow chilies, I can sow my spring onions, I can sow spinach, kale, lettuce, all of them. But it is important to know that you want to do this 24 to 48 hours before the aspect. So on the biodynamic calendar, you'll see the time as well as the day when this occurs.

Plan your garden tasks to occur between 24-48 hours before the Moon opposition to Saturn aspect."

Name withheld

Understanding Lunar Nodes:
The Cosmic Pause Button for Gardeners

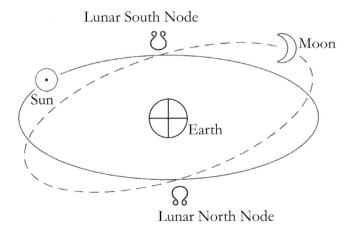

In the celestial ballet of the Moon and the Sun, there are moments when their paths intersect. These points of intersection are called lunar nodes. For gardeners who practice biodynamics, these nodes are more than just astronomical footnotes; they are significant influences that can disrupt plant growth and seed germination.

The Unpredictable Nature of Nodes

The influence of nodes on biodynamic gardening is debated both in duration and intensity. Some experts propose that the effects can linger for two hours before and four hours after the precise moment when the Moon's path crosses that of the Sun. Others argue for a window of four hours before and two hours after. So we want to avoid any garden work around the time of the node as it will gradually come into effect and gradually depart.

During these periods, it's best to refrain from sowing seeds, transplanting seedlings, or carrying out any other significant gardening tasks that could affect the life cycle of your plants.

Built-In Rest Days

One of the beautiful aspects of lunar nodes in the context of biodynamic gardening is that they serve as natural rest days—think of them as the cosmic pause button for both you and your garden. When you consult your biodynamic gardening calendar, you'll notice that usually two node events occur in a calendar month.

The Philosophy of Rest and Growth

The thing that biodynamic practitioners love the most about nodes, is that they're rest days. Nature has built in rest in our garden. Nature itself has an ebb and flow, a rhythm of exertion and rest that all living things—including plants and humans—are a part of. Recognizing and respecting these natural cycles allows us to garden in a way that's more harmonious with the Earth's own rhythms.

What is Perigee and Apogee?

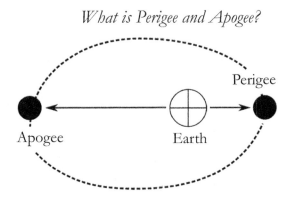

Perigee and apogee refer to the changing distance between the Moon and Earth due to the Moon's elliptical orbit. Perigee is the point in the Moon's orbit where it is closest to the Earth, while apogee is the point where it is furthest from the Earth.

These aspects of the Moon's orbit can have an influence on plants, generally resulting in unbalanced or weaker growth. However, it's worth noting that potatoes are an exception and are believed to be best planted during the apogee.

When it comes to gardening tasks, it is recommended to avoid working during the times of perigee and apogee, just like you will avoid garden tasks during the node aspect.

CHAPTER 4:

It's All About the Soil—From pH Levels to Microbial Health

Now that we have explored some of the more nuanced biodynamic gardening methods relating to the Moon the stars and the constellations, we're going to dive back into broader organic and sustainable gardening methods to complement your Moon gardening practice.

The Bedrock of Health: Understanding Soil pH
Your well-being is inextricably linked to the health of the soil in which your food grows. A seasoned gardener will tell you that soil is not just the earth beneath your feet but the foundation upon which the garden's vitality rests.

Before diving into your gardening activities, it's crucial to test your soil's pH levels and nutrient profile. Soil pH, the measure of how acidic or alkaline it is, significantly influences both plant health and microbial activity.

Ideally, garden soil should have a pH ranging from 6.0 to 7.0, spanning from slightly acidic to neutral. This range allows most plants to effectively absorb essential nutrients. Some plants, like blueberries, prefer more acidic conditions (pH 4.0–5.5), while others, such as asparagus, lean towards alkaline soil (pH 7.0–8.0). Therefore, it's vital to know the specific needs of the plants you intend to cultivate.

Amending Soil pH:
◊ **Adding Lime:** This natural soil amendment raises the pH of acidic soils towards the neutral range.
◊ **Adding Sulfur:** Sulfur can be used to lower the pH of alkaline soils, making them more acidic.
◊ **Organic Matter:** Organic materials like compost, peat moss, or well-rotted manure can gradually balance pH levels and enrich the soil.

Soil Types: Know Your Ground
Soil can vary widely, and understanding your soil type can significantly impact your gardening success. Here are some commonly found soil types in American gardens:
◊ **Clay Soil:** Heavy and dense, clay soil retains moisture but can become waterlogged, leading to root rot.
◊ **Sandy Soil:** Light and porous, sandy soil drains quickly but doesn't hold nutrients or moisture well.
◊ **Loam Soil:** The gold standard of gardening soils, loam is a balanced mix of sand, clay, and organic matter, providing excellent drainage and fertility.
◊ **Peat Soil:** Dark and acidic, peat soil is rich in organic matter and retains moisture well. It's great for specific

plants like blueberries and cranberries.

◊ **Rocky Soil:** Found in mountainous regions, rocky soil is well-drained but challenging to work with. It's rich in minerals but may require substantial amendment for gardening.

Cultivating Soil Microbes: The Unsung Heroes of Your Garden

Taking care of your soil isn't just about feeding your plants; it's about nurturing an entire ecosystem. Microorganisms like bacteria, fungi, and micro-arthropods play a critical role in soil health. They break down organic matter into plant-accessible nutrients and help maintain soil structure, allowing for adequate air and water circulation.

To foster a healthy microbial community:

◊ **Add Organic Matter:** Compost and other organic materials improve soil structure and provide essential nutrients.

◊ **Mulching:** A layer of mulch helps conserve moisture and regulates soil temperature, creating a conducive environment for microbial life.

◊ **Sustainable Practices:** Avoid over-tilling and the use of synthetic chemicals, both of which can disrupt microbial communities.

Microorganisms in the soil form a symbiotic relationship with plants. During particular Moon phases, these activities may be more pronounced, making it an ideal time to add compost or other organic material to your soil.

Understanding and improving soil quality isn't just about immediate yield; it's a long-term investment in the ecosystem of your garden and, by extension, your own health. In Moon gardening, you're not just following age-old traditions or folklore; you're integrating science, ancestral wisdom, and observational skill to create a holistic gardening practice.

CHAPTER 5:

Make my Garden Grow

When you plant your seeds or seedlings it might now feel as though you've reached the end of a journey. However this is just the beginning of a rewarding experience. Your fledgling plants now need consistent and thoughtful care to mature into a fruitful garden. One essential practice that harmonizes wonderfully with lunar cycles or other gardening methods you may be using is mulching.

Benefits of Mulching

Why is mulching so crucial, you ask? Well, it offers a myriad of benefits that help create a hospitable environment where your plants can truly flourish. Firstly, mulch serves as a moisture-retaining blanket for your soil, especially during the sweltering summer months or in regions where water is a limited resource. By locking in moisture, mulch ensures your plants remain hydrated and less prone to drying out.

Weed Control: A mulch layer minimizes the sprouting of weeds by blocking sunlight. This leaves your plants to grow in a more stress-free environment.

Temperature Moderation: Mulch acts as an insulator, keeping the soil cool during hot days and warm during cooler weather, providing a stable environment for root systems.

Nutrient Addition: Organic mulches decompose over time, enriching the soil with essential nutrients. This contributes to a healthy, thriving garden ecosystem.

Erosion Prevention: Mulch serves as a protective barrier, minimizing the impact of heavy rains and strong winds that can erode the topsoil.

Pest and Disease Mitigation: Certain types of mulch like cedar chips have natural oils that act as pest repellents. This can be an additional line of defense against garden pests and diseases.

Step-by-Step Guide to Mulching

Choose Your Mulch: Organic options like bark chips, straw, and compost are ideal for gardens focusing on sustainability. Inorganic options like gravel and rubber chips may be suitable for specific landscaping needs.

Preparation is Key: Clear away any weeds, stones, or other debris from the area you intend to mulch. Watering the soil lightly can also make the mulch more effective in retaining moisture.

Application: Apply a 2-3 inch layer of your chosen mulch material, making sure to leave some space around the base of each plant. This prevents rot and allows the plant to breathe.

Ongoing Maintenance: Organic mulch decomposes over time; so you'll need to replenish it periodically. If you notice that the mulch has become compacted, aerate it with a garden fork to allow better water penetration.

Timing is key when it comes to nourishing your Moon garden plants. It's considered optimal to fertilize during the waxing phase, when the Moon gets bigger. The energy from the growing Moon will support plant growth by making it easier for them to absorb the nutrients they need to thrive.

A well-made compost, particularly if it contains animal manures, meets most, if not all, of a soil's nutrient needs and most Moon gardeners add some every growing season. Sometimes though, the ground may need supplementary fertilizer throughout the summer due to nutrient deficiencies. Some examples of organic fertilizers for use in a Moon garden include:

◊ **Manure:** Animal manures such as chicken, cow, or horse manure are rich in nitrogen, phosphorus, and potassium—all essential compounds for plant growth.

◊ **Blood meal:** This fertilizer is made from dried and ground animal blood and is a good nitrogen source.

◊ **Fish emulsion:** Made from processed fish, this fertilizer is a good source of nitrogen, phosphorus and potassium.

◊ **Bone meal:** Made from ground animal bones, this fertilizer is high in phosphorus and is ideal for promoting strong root development.

◊ **Rock phosphate:** This fertilizer is made from ground rock and is a slow-release source of phosphorus.

◊ **Alfalfa meal:** This fertilizer is made from dehydrated alfalfa leaves and is a good source of nitrogen, phosphorus, and potassium, as well as several other micronutrients.

◊ **Kelp meal:** Made from seaweed, kelp meal is a good source of several essential nutrients, including nitrogen, phosphorus, and potassium.

◊ **Green sand:** This fertilizer is made from crushed marine minerals and is a good source of several essential micronutrients.

◊ **Vermicompost:** Also called worm castings, vermicompost is made from worm poop and is a rich source of several essential nutrients.

No matter which organic fertilizer you use, make sure you follow the recommended application rates and to incorporate the fertilizer into the soil for maximum efficacy.

Making Organic Compost

While it's possible to purchase premade compost from most garden stores, making your own can be rewarding. I love my compost heap! It is such a great way to use up kitchen vegetable waste, dead leaves in autumn, grass clippings and general garden waste. Here's a simple recipe for getting started:

Ingredients:
- ◊ Brown materials (leaves, twigs, branches, straw)
- ◊ Green materials (grass clippings, kitchen scraps, coffee grounds)
- ◊ Water

Instructions:
- ◊ Start by creating a compost bin or pile in a sunny location. You can purchase a compost bin or create a simple pile using stakes or bricks.
- ◊ Alternately layer green and brown materials in the compost bin or pile, starting with a layer of brown materials, then a layer of green materials, and so on.
- ◊ Moisten each layer of materials as you build your compost pile, ensuring the materials are damp but not soaked.
- ◊ Turn the compost pile every two to three weeks using a garden fork or shovel. This will help to aerate the pile and speed up the decomposition process.
- ◊ Continue to add materials to your compost pile as they become available.
- ◊ Keep the pile moist by ensuring it gets rained on or occasionally spraying it down with a hose.

After several months, your compost should be fully decomposed and ready to use in your garden. Good compost feels crumbly and has a grainy texture, like soil that's been broken down. It should be a little damp, but not too wet or dry. When you smell it, it should have a nice earthy scent, similar to fresh soil. The color of good compost is usually dark brown or black, showing that it's gone through the decomposition process. You won't find big chunks of stuff that hasn't broken down yet; it should be all broken up into tiny pieces. Just remember, to get good compost texture, you need to use the right ingredients, give it enough air, and turn it regularly.

My secret ingredient that makes for amazing compost is the addition of finely ground zeolite. Zeolite is a simple clay used for cat litter, it is highly absorbent and eliminates odours effectively. I add a cupful of zeolite to my compost bin every week or so. This silica-based environmentally friendly mineral detoxifies the soil, curbs leaching and acts as a strong fertilizer booster.

By using compost in your garden, you can improve the health and productivity of your plants and reduce your impact on the environment by reducing the amount of organic waste sent to landfills. Happy composting!

Growing and Using Comfrey

Comfrey is a hardy perennial herb that is easy to grow and care for. It is a crucial part of any successful garden and is used as a compost activator or as a "chop-and-drop" mulch. Comfrey is not particularly fussy about soil conditions, but it does prefer well-drained soil with a slightly acidic to neutral pH range of 6.0 to 7.0. The plant likes full sun but can tolerate partial shade. Ensure that the chosen site is where you want the comfrey to remain for a long time, as it has a deep taproot and can be difficult to eradicate completely once established!

You can start comfrey from seed, but it's usually quicker and more reliable to plant root cuttings or offsets (baby plants that grow at the base of a mature plant).

Harvest comfrey leaves as you need them. It's often best to allow the plant to grow for its first year without harvesting to ensure it establishes well.

After that, you can harvest leaves as needed, ideally before the plant flowers for best leaf potency. It's one of the most beneficial plants you can grow and it can be used in so many ways:

◊ **Nutrient Content:** Comfrey is known for its high nutrient content, which makes it an excellent source of organic fertilizer for your garden plants. Comfrey leaves are high in nitrogen, phosphorus, and potassium, making it an effective fertilizer for both flowers and vegetables.

◊ **Soil Improvement:** Comfrey has a deep root system that helps to improve soil structure and fertility. The roots of the comfrey plant can reach down several feet into the soil, bringing up nutrients from deep within the earth. This makes comfrey a great addition to a Moon garden, where you want to create a soil environment rich in nutrients and conducive to plant growth.

◊ **Pest Deterrent:** Comfrey is also known to repel certain pests and diseases, making it a natural pest control option for your Moon garden.

◊ **Companion Planting:** Comfrey is a great companion plant. Its deep roots help to keep the soil healthy, and its leaves can be used to make compost tea to nourish other plants.

Comfrey Tea Fertilizer

Comfrey tea is natural fertilizer that is easy to make and can provide your garden with essential nutrients. Here's a simple recipe for making comfrey tea:

Ingredients:
Fresh comfrey leaves
Water

Instructions:
◊ Harvest fresh comfrey leaves from your comfrey plants, or gather comfrey leaves from a local source.

◊ Fill a large container, such as a barrel or trash can, with fresh comfrey leaves.
◊ Fill the container with water, ensuring the comfrey leaves are entirely submerged.
◊ Cover the container and let it sit in a sunny location for several weeks until the comfrey leaves have broken down and the water has turned dark and rich.
◊ Strain the comfrey tea through a fine mesh strainer to remove any debris.
◊ Dilute the comfrey tea with water before using, at a ratio of one part comfrey tea to five parts water.
◊ Use the comfrey tea as a fertilizer, either by watering it directly onto the soil around your plants, or by mixing it into the soil before planting.

Here is recipe for a seaweed and comfrey liquid fertilizer that can be used to supplement your garden's nutrient needs. Rich in nitrogen, so ideal for greedy feeders such as cabbages, leeks and tomatoes, Do not use this on beans or peas.

Comfrey and Seaweed Liquid Fertilizer

Ingredients:
2 cups of fresh or dried seaweed
2 cups of comfrey leaves
Water

Instructions:
◊ Rinse the seaweed and comfrey leaves to remove any dirt or debris.
◊ lace the seaweed and comfrey leaves in a large, lidded container.
◊ Fill the container with water, ensuring the seaweed and comfrey leaves are entirely submerged.
◊ Allow the mixture to steep for at least two weeks. The longer it steeps, the more potent the fertilizer will be.
◊ Strain the mixture through a fine mesh sieve to remove the solid materials.

The liquid fertilizer can be stored in an airtight container for up to six months. To use, dilute the liquid fertilizer with water at a ratio of 1:10 before applying it to your garden.

Note: Always use caution when applying any fertilizer to your plants. Over-fertilizing can be harmful to your plants and the environment.

How To Use a Green Manure in the Fall

If you want to try an alternative to compost, consider growing green manure. Green manure is a practice of sowing certain plants specifically to dig them back into the soil, which improves soil structure, boosts fertility, and even helps to suppress weeds. Most are legumes like clover or alfalfa, but plants like rye or mustard also work well.

To start a green manure, choose a planting location in your garden and prepare the soil by removing any weeds or debris. It's usually best to plant in autumn so the seeds can sprout over winter. Scatter the seeds of your chosen green manure crop over the area and lightly rake them in. Make sure to follow the recommended planting depth and spacing on the seed packet.

In the spring, you can simply cut the plants down at soil level before they go to seed and till them back into the soil. This will help to break down the plant material and add organic matter to the soil, improving its structure and fertility.

Green manures can be especially beneficial in small urban gardens where space is limited. By rotating your crops and planting green manure in between rotations you can help to maintain healthy soil and improve the overall health of your garden.

Many biodynamic practioners practice a no-dig gardening method, so as not to disrupt the soil structure, so they don't dig the manure crop back in to the soil, rather cut it down and lay the cuttings on the bed before layering the bed with other materials depending on what crop is going to be grown next.

CHAPTER 6:

Watering Wisely

Water is the lifeblood of any garden, but it's also a finite and precious resource that should be used responsibly. The symbiotic relationship between water and plant growth is significant, and sometimes, it's all about timing. In lunar gardening, for example, timing your watering can make all the difference.

Waxing Moon: The period of the waxing Moon, when the Moon appears to be growing in the sky, is believed to be a time of expansion and growth. It is during this phase that you should focus on watering your plants. The gravitational pull from the waxing Moon is thought to improve water absorption and retention by the soil and plants, encouraging vigorous growth.

Waning Moon: Conversely, the waning Moon phase, when the Moon appears to be shrinking, is the perfect time for adding fertilizers or other soil amendments. During this phase, the Moon's energies are said to encourage the soil to absorb nutrients more efficiently, thus making your fertilization efforts more effective.

Being mindful of water consumption is not just an eco-friendly choice; it can also translate to cost savings on your water bill. Here are some strategies to make every drop count:

Select Drought-Resistant Plants: Opt for plant varieties that are well-adapted to drier conditions. These plants will require less frequent watering, conserving water in the long run.

Invest in Mulching: As discussed in an earlier chapter, mulch serves multiple purposes. It keeps the soil moist by reducing the rate of evaporation, thereby lessening the need for frequent watering.

Deep, Infrequent Watering: Rather than light, daily watering, opt for a deep and thorough soaking less frequently (e.g., once or twice a week). This encourages the roots to grow deeper into the soil, making the plant more resilient during dry spells.

Harvest Rainwater: Setting up a rain barrel or another rainwater collection system can provide you with a supply of 'free' water. Not only does this save money, but rainwater is also generally better for plants because it doesn't contain the minerals found in tap water.

Avoid Midday Watering: Watering during the peak heat of the day can result in significant water loss due to evaporation. It's best to water your plants in the early morning. This approach minimizes evaporation and allows plants to take up water before the heat of the day, while also helping to prevent fungal diseases that can proliferate when plants are wet overnight.

CHAPTER 7:

Pest Management

Pests can be a problem in any garden and Moon gardens are no exception. As Moon gardening is a holistic practice, it is important to avoid using harsh chemicals that can harm the environment or the beneficial insects you want to encourage.

The Basics of Pest Control
Understanding the pests that frequent your garden is the first step in environmentally friendly pest control. Not all insects are detrimental; many are beneficial for the garden's ecosystem, playing roles in pollination and natural pest control. In the spirit of Moon gardening, the focus is on maintaining a balanced environment where plants and animals can coexist sustainably. If pests do become problematic, there are a multitude of natural remedies you can apply before resorting to chemical options.

One such natural alternative is a homemade vinegar spray, which is effective for treating various common garden pests like aphids and spider mites. Below is a simple recipe you can prepare at home:

Ingredients:
1 cup white vinegar
1 cup water
2 tablespoons dish soap (preferably eco-friendly)

Instructions:
Combine the white vinegar, water, and dish soap in a large spray bottle. Seal the bottle and shake well to thoroughly mix the ingredients. Before you go all-in, it's crucial to test the spray on a small, inconspicuous section of the affected plant. Observe for any adverse reactions over 24 hours. Once you've determined the spray is safe for your plants, proceed to generously spray the mixture on the infested areas of the plants, paying special attention to both sides of the leaves and the stems. Reapply the mixture once a week or as needed, observing the pest levels to determine the efficacy of the treatment.
Note: Be cautious when applying the vinegar spray so as not to harm beneficial insects like ladybugs, lacewings, and bees, who are valuable allies in your garden.

If necessary, you can also use natural pest control products like neem oil or vinegar sprays.

About Neem Oil
Neem oil is a natural pesticide that is derived from the seeds of the neem tree. It has a long history of use as a pest control in agriculture. Here are the steps to use neem oil for controlling pests in gardening:
   ◊   Purchase pure, cold-pressed neem oil from a garden
        center or online retailer.
   ◊   Mix the neem oil with water according to the product
        label's instructions. Typically, the ratio is one to two
        ounces of neem oil per gallon of water.
   ◊   Add a few drops of dish soap to the mixture to help
        it stick to the leaves of the plants.
   ◊   Fill a garden sprayer with the neem oil mixture and
        shake well to mix.
   ◊   Spray the mixture onto the affected plants, covering

every part, including the undersides of leaves where pests often hide.

◊ Repeat the application every seven to ten days or as needed until the pests are under control.

Note: It is crucial to test the neem oil spray on a small, inconspicuous area of the plant before applying it to the entire plant to ensure it won't cause any damage. Also, be careful not to spray the mixture on beneficial insects like ladybugs or bees.

Beneficial Insects

Beneficial insects are the unsung heroes in your garden's mini-ecosystem, serving critical roles that go beyond mere pest control. Not only do they help keep troublesome pests in check, but they also aid in pollination and soil aeration, contributing to a healthier and more productive garden. Embracing these insects can significantly reduce your dependency on chemical pesticides, fostering a more sustainable and ecologically balanced gardening approach.

A Closer Look at Beneficial Insects You'll Want in Your Garden

Here's a rundown of some commonly found beneficial insects, their roles, and why you would want to welcome them into your garden:

Ladybugs: More than just charming garden ornaments, ladybugs are voracious eaters of aphids, scale insects, and other soft-bodied pests. They are quite effective at protecting plants like roses and vegetables from infestations, devouring thousands of aphids in their lifetime.

Lacewings: Known for their delicate, transparent wings, lacewings are a friend to gardeners for their predatory skills. Lacewing larvae consume a range of pests, including aphids, mites, and thrips. Adults, while primarily pollen feeders, continue to consume pests in smaller quantities.

Parasitic Wasps: The term "parasitic wasps" might sound intimidating, but these insects are actually allies. They lay their eggs inside caterpillars, aphids, or other insect pests. As the eggs hatch, the larvae consume their host from the inside, effectively reducing the pest population without harming your plants.

Bees: Perhaps the most universally adored beneficial insects, bees are pollination champions. Without them, the yield and quality of fruits, vegetables, and flowering plants would significantly drop. Bees help in the fertilization process, ensuring robust, flavorful harvests.

Spiders: Often misunderstood, spiders serve as natural predators in the garden. They feed on a multitude of pests, including aphids, mites, and flies. Some spiders even build intricate webs to trap flying insects, providing an aesthetic bonus along with their pest control benefits.

Cultivating a Friendly Environment for Beneficial Insects
Creating a welcoming habitat for these beneficial insects can go a long way in maintaining a balanced and thriving garden. Some ways to attract and support them include:

Provide habitat space: Create good living conditions for beneficial insects by planting various flowers, shrubs, and trees that provide food and shelter. Flowers with small, shallow blooms, such as daisies, are particularly attractive to many beneficial insects.

Avoid pesticides: Chemical pesticides can kill both pests and beneficial insects, so avoid using them in the garden. Instead, use natural pest control methods, such as neem oil or vinegar sprays.

Ensure water access: Provide a shallow dish of water with pebbles or sticks so that beneficial insects can drink.

Minimize tillage: Refrain from working the soil in the garden, as this can disrupt the habitat of beneficial insects and soil organisms.

Provide food sources: Ensure plenty of nectar and pollen are available by planting various flowering plants throughout the growing season.

By following these tips, you can create a garden that's both friendly to beneficial insects and supportive of the larger ecosystem. In turn, these insects will help to control pests and promote healthy plant growth in your Moon garden.

Keeping Diseases at Bay

Be on the lookout for the signs of disease on your plants, including these three common types:

◊ Powdery mildew: white powder on leaves
◊ Black spot: yellowing leaves covered with black spots, the leaves then drop, common on roses
◊ Rust: rusty brown spots on leaves can also affect your Moon garden plants and quickly spread and cause significant damage to your Moon garden

Soil-borne Diseases: diseases such as clubroot and verticillium wilt can be more challenging to manage as they reside in the soil and can persist for several years. The best way to manage them is to avoid planting crops in any soil that was infected over the past three years. Following a crop rotation plan is a good way to do this naturally.

An old gardener's trick to curb clubroot in cabbages? Bury a few rhubarb stems in the soil before you plant them.

Poor Yields: If your Moon garden is not producing the yields you expect, it may be due to poor soil quality, lack of sunlight, or an incorrect planting time. To improve yields, make sure your plants are getting adequate sunlight, and amend your soil with compost or other organic matter to improve its quality.

Good Garden Practices

Good garden practices form the cornerstone of a successful and sustainable gardening experience and serves as a first line of defense against various diseases and pests. To prevent the spread of diseases, it is important to practice good garden hygiene, such as:

◊ Removing infected leaves or plants. Burn them—don't add them to your compost heap! Dormant spores within the infected material can contaminate the compost and reintroduce the disease into your soil when you use it.
◊ Avoiding overhead watering. This can spread fragments of diseases throughout the growing space.

◊ Consider using disease-resistant varieties, rotating crops, and improving soil health with compost or mulch.

How to do Crop Rotation

Crop rotation is a method of growing different crops in a planned sequence over several growing seasons to maintain soil health and prevent disease and pest problems.

In a small urban garden, crop rotation can be achieved by dividing the garden into different sections and rotating the crops between them each year. Rotating crops can prevent soil depletion and ensures the nutrients in the soil do not become exhausted or disease prone. This is typically done in a three or four-year cycle.

By rotating the crops in this way, the soil can replenish nutrients that are depleted by each crop family while also reducing the build-up of soil-borne diseases and pests that can affect a specific crop.

Here's one example of a crop rotation planting plan:

◊ In the first year, plant brassicas such as kale, broccoli, and cauliflower.
◊ In the second year, plant legumes like beans and peas in that same section.
◊ In the third year, plant nightshades such as tomatoes.
◊ In the fourth year, finish the rotation with root crops such as carrots, onions, and potatoes.

Boost the benefits of crop rotation further by adding compost or organic matter to the soil each year. This can further improve soil health and fertility, which will ultimately lead to better yields and healthier plants.

CHAPTER 8:

Companion Planting

Plants, like people, do best in a village. In other words, your garden will thrive when it's home to an abundance of plant varieties that complement each other. Companion planting is a practice that pairs specific plants together to create mutually beneficial relationships, improving growth, deterring pests, and sometimes even enhancing flavor.

Companion planting and Moon gardening are both techniques that seek harmony with nature's rhythms. When you combine these lunar rhythms with companion planting, you can significantly magnify the benefits of both. Below are some common companion planting techniques for a variety of vegetables, herbs, and flowers.

Vegetables:

Tomatoes
- ◊   **Companion Plants:** Basil, oregano and marigolds.
- ◊   **Benefits:** Basil and oregano help deter tomato pests, and marigolds ward off nematodes.

Carrots
◊ Companion Plants: Rosemary, chives, and tomatoes.
◊ Benefits: These companions help repel the carrot fly.

Cucumbers
◊ Companion Plants: Corn, beans, and nasturtium.
◊ Benefits: Corn provides shade, beans add nitrogen to the soil, and nasturtiums deter pests.

Lettuce
◊ Companion Plants: Radishes, carrots and strawberries.
◊ Benefits: Radishes can help deter aphids, while carrots and strawberries are neutral companions that co-exist well.

Peppers
◊ Companion Plants: Basil, onions, and spinach.
◊ Benefits: Basil helps deter pests, and onions and spinach are neutral companions.

Herbs:

Basil
◊ Companion Plants: Tomatoes and peppers.
◊ Benefits: Helps deter pests from these vegetables.

Rosemary
◊ Companion Plants: Beans, cabbage and carrots.
◊ Benefits: Repels bean beetles, cabbage moths and carrot flies.

Mint
◊ Companion Plants: Cabbage and tomatoes.
◊ Benefits: Deters cabbage moths and ants.

Dill
◊ Companion Plants: Cabbage, onions and lettuce.
◊ Benefits: Attracts beneficial insects and can help repel aphids.

Flowers:

Marigolds
- ◊ Companion Plants: Almost all vegetables.
- ◊ Benefits: Deters nematodes and other soil pests.

Nasturtiums
- ◊ Companion Plants: Cucumbers, zucchinis, and pumpkins.
- ◊ Benefits: Deters squash bugs, cucumber beetles, and aphids.

Lavender
- ◊ Companion Plants: Cabbage, broccoli, and other brassicas.
- ◊ Benefits: Deters moths and other pests.

Sunflowers
- ◊ Companion Plants: Cucumbers, squash, and pumpkins.
- ◊ Benefits: Provides climbing support and attracts pollinators.

Companion planting can be used to create a microclimate that is suitable for specific crops. Planting tall crops like corn near shorter crops like beans can provide shade and reduce the risk of moisture loss.

Don't be afraid to experiment with different arrangements of companion plants. Try various combinations of companion plants and observe the results to determine which combinations work best in your growing space.

Remember, companion planting is as much an art as it is a science and results may vary depending on local conditions. Nonetheless, these traditional techniques offer a natural approach to managing pests, optimizing space, and improving garden health. It's a simple step to take that can make a noticeable difference.

CHAPTER 9:

Growing Common Vegetables
using Lunar and Biodynamic Gardening Methods

N ow that you have the secrets of lunar planting at your finger-
tips, let's bring it all together to guide you through growing
some of our most common vegetables.

Potatoes

When to Plant: The best time to plant potatoes is during root days, specifically on a waning or descending Moon. Aim for mid-March to mid-May,
depending on your region's climate and soil conditions.

How to Plant: Dig trenches or holes approximately 7cm deep, spaced
about 50cm apart within rows, and place rows about 50cm apart from each
other. The waning Moon's gravitational pull supports better root development, setting the stage for healthier plants.

When to Fertilize: Apply fertilizer during the waning Moon, a time when plants are less likely to grow spindly and are more focused on root development.

How to Fertilize: Ideally, prepare the beds in Autumn so they can benefit from natural soil decomposition over the winter. Alternatively, fill the trenches or holes with well-rotted compost. This practice will align with the Moon's waning phase, promoting healthier, stronger roots.

Moisture: Keep the soil moist, particularly when the plants are flowering. The waning Moon's lower gravitational pull will aid in water retention.

When to Harvest: Aim for Root days during a descending Moon phase for optimal storage longevity. This period aligns with when the leaves turn yellow, signaling that the potatoes are ready for harvest.

Pro Tips: Seed Potatoes: Always opt for blight-resistant seed potatoes to safeguard against disease.

Chitting: To encourage sprouting, chit your seed potatoes before planting. Expose them to light, avoiding direct sunlight, with their eyes facing upwards. The stored energy will give them a healthy start, further aligning your planting efforts with the Moon's beneficial phases.

Broccoli

When to sow seed: The ideal time to sow broccoli seeds is on flower days when the Moon is in its waxing phase, a period known for promoting vegetative growth. For outdoor sowing, aim for late March or April when the soil has started to warm up. If you're starting your seeds indoors, you can begin a bit earlier, in late winter. Prepare your soil with well-drained compost and sow your seeds about 5 cm deep, placing 2-3 seeds every 10 cm in rows. To boost germination rates, consider soaking the seeds in warm water for a few hours before sowing.

Planting and Spacing: Transplant your seedlings or plant your seeds directly into the ground, again favoring flower days, but this time look for a descending Moon, which is believed to encourage root development. Plant your seedlings or space your rows about 30 cm apart to give each broccoli plant ample room to grow and spread.

When to fertilize: Fertilize your broccoli on flower days when the Moon is waning, as this phase is thought to be good for soil absorption and root growth. Broccoli plants are heavy feeders and will benefit from a balanced fertilizer, along with regular applications of compost or mulch to help retain soil moisture.

Harvesting: Wait for another flower day to harvest your broccoli. Cut the main head along with a portion of the stem. Make sure to harvest before the flowers on the head start to bloom for the best flavor and texture. You can continue to harvest smaller side shoots for several weeks after the main head has been cut.

ProTips: Soaking seeds in warm water before sowing can accelerate the germination process. Keep an eye out for slugs and other pests.

Tomatoes

When to Sow: The waxing Moon phase, particularly on fruit days, is considered optimal for sowing tomato seeds, as this Moon phase promotes the growth of above-ground plant parts. Starting your seeds indoors around late February or early March at temperatures between 70-75°F (21-24°C) will give you a head start on the growing season. If you can provide these conditions, your seeds will germinate more successfully.

Planting and Spacing: Wait until the danger of the last frost has passed before transplanting your tomato seedlings outdoors. For the best results, aim to plant on fruit days during a descending Moon, a period traditionally believed to encourage root development. Tomatoes thrive in a sunny, sheltered spot and will require support structures like stakes or cages to help them grow vertically. Make sure to plant the seedlings deep to encourage a strong root system.

When to Fertilize: Do so on fruit days during a waning Moon. The waning Moon is said to enhance the soil's absorption capacity, aiding the plants in taking up nutrients. Tomatoes are heavy feeders and will benefit greatly from a soil rich in organic matter. Generously apply compost or well-rotted manure and keep the soil consistently moist throughout the growing season.

Harvesting: Harvest your tomatoes on ascending Moon days that also fall on fruit days for the best results. The ascending Moon is thought to draw plant energies upward, which may contribute to a juicier, more flavorful fruit. If you have any green tomatoes left on the vine towards the end of the season, you can allow them to ripen indoors, covered with a cloth.

Pro Tips: Mulching with comfrey leaves or even tomato leaves can help to retain soil moisture and deter weeds.
   ◊   Avoid planting tomatoes next to potatoes, as they are more susceptible to similar diseases.
   ◊   As autumn approaches, pinch off the tops of the plants in September. This stops further leaf growth and allows the plant to focus its energy on ripening existing fruit.

Salad and Leafy Greens

When to Sow: For leafy greens like spinach, lettuce, or Swiss chard, consider sowing your seeds on leaf days during a waxing Moon. The waxing Moon is traditionally believed to favor the growth of leaves and stems. Start your seeds indoors under glass from February to March or directly outside from April through the end of July, depending on your climate and the specific crop.

Transplanting and Spacing: The best time for transplanting your leafy greens outdoors is on leaf days during a descending Moon. This lunar phase is thought to encourage strong root development. Planting in the evening or on a cloudy day can minimize transplant shock and help the young plants adapt to their new environment. When transplanting, be mindful of the root length; you can clip longer roots to make planting easier. Make sure not to plant them too deeply.

Soil and Fertilization: Leafy greens generally don't require heavy fertilization, but they do appreciate a well-composted soil. Aim to hoe your garden on leaf days to disrupt weed growth and encourage soil aeration without the need for extra fertilizers.

Harvesting: For the freshest flavor, harvest your leafy greens in the morning. If you're growing loose-leaf varieties, you can pick small leaves as needed, providing a continual harvest.

Pro Tips: Keep the soil consistently moist to ensure optimal growing conditions.

◊ Be vigilant for slugs, which can quickly decimate leafy greens; consider using natural deterrents if needed.
◊ Hoe your garden regularly to keep weeds at bay.
◊ Avoid planting your leafy greens next to parsley, as they can be incompatible neighbors in the garden.

CHAPTER 10:

How to Improve your Garden Connection

Before diving hands-first into the soil and embarking on your gardening journey, it's essential to pause and build a deeper connection with your natural surroundings. So, let's step back for a moment and lay the groundwork for a more mindful and fulfilling gardening experience. By learning how to be better in tune with nature, you can improve your ability to make the kinds of choices that most benefit it.

Learn the Skill of Observation

Observation is a crucial aspect of Moon gardening and biodynamics. It allows us to closely monitor our plants and the environment they are growing in. When you make detailed observations of the natural world, you will have a better idea of the ways dozens of factors work together to affect your garden.

Observation puts you in the drivers seat to take notice and detect early warning signs of plant diseases, insect infestations, and other issues that could affect the health and growth of our plants. Observing the behavior of the wildlife around us can also provide insight into the health of the ecosystem and help us make informed decisions about how to manage our garden. Additionally, observation lets us understand the unique conditions of our garden, such as sunlight, soil type, and water availability and make adjustments to our gardening practices accordingly. Here are some suggestions about how you can improve your ability to observe:

Take a "Five-Senses" Nature Walk

Much like the idea's of the Japanese method of "forest bathing," a five senses nature walk helps you get anchored in your space. Walk through your garden five times, focusing on using a different sense each time.

During the first walk
Use your sense of SIGHT to closely observe the colors, textures, and shapes of the plants. Take note of any changes or differences since your last walk.
During the second walk
Use your sense of SMELL to explore the fragrances of the flowers and herbs in your garden. Crush leaves and turn over the soil and smell it, immerse yourself in the garden's bouquet.
During the third walk
Use your sense of TOUCH to feel the different textures of the plants, the soil, and any other objects in your garden. Notice the roughness of tree bark, the softness of flower petals, and the coolness of a leafy canopy. Absorb the tactile tapestry of your garden.
During the fourth walk
Use your sense of HEARING to listen to the sounds of nature around you. Close your eyes and open your ears. Pay attention to the rustling of leaves in the wind, the chirping of birds and the buzzing of insects.
During the fifth walk
Use your sense of TASTE to sample the fruits, vegetables, or herbs growing in your garden. Taste a fresh tomato or an edible leaf, and savor the flavors around you.

By taking five walks, each with a different focus, you may develop a more profound connection to your garden and the natural world. Mindfully using all of our senses can help us better engage with our surroundings and also help to reduce stress, boost mood, and improve overall well-being.

84

You can complete the exercise by taking a sixth walk that integrates all your senses. Reflect on the emotions or inspirations that the previous walks evoked. Become aware of any extra sensations, emotions, feelings, or memories you have beyond your physical body.

Keep a Moon Gardeners Journal

Keeping a Moon gardening journal is another useful gardening tool. Not only will you learn to observe more closely, this is also a place to record and reflect on your successes, failures, aspirations, and plans.

How you keep a journal is up to you. The entries can be as simple as the weather or as complex as daily check-ins on the lunar positions in the sky. It only takes a few months of notes to begin seeing patterns and looking forward to the next observation.

Many of history's greatest gardeners have kept a meticulous record of activities and events in their growing spaces. They noted all pertinent information about their flowers, fruit trees and vegetables, including varieties and sowing places, harvesting times and overall weather conditions.

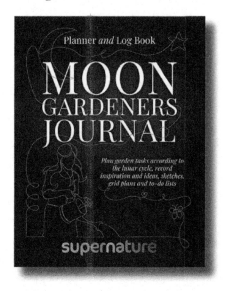

Ideas for your Journal:

Daily Observations: Take note of the weather conditions, such as temperature, sunlight and rainfall. Record any changes you notice in your plants, such as new growth, blooming flowers, or signs of pests or diseases. Document the interactions you observe between different plant species or between plants and wildlife.

Garden Tasks: Track the tasks you perform in your garden, such as planting, watering, pruning, or fertilizing. Note down any challenges you encounter, like soil issues, weeds, or unexpected setbacks. Reflect on the techniques or strategies you try and their effectiveness.

Personal Reflections: Use your garden journal as a space for self-reflection. Write about the emotions and moods you experience while tending to your garden. Express your joys, frustrations, and moments of awe. Reflect on how your garden impacts your well-being and overall connection with nature.

Inspirations and Ideas: Jot down any inspirations or creative ideas that come to you while in the garden. It could be a new planting combination, a garden design concept, or a DIY project. Use your journal as a repository for brainstorming and exploring new possibilities for your garden.

Lessons Learned: Reflect on the lessons you've learned through your gardening experiences. Write about the successes and failures, and what you've discovered about plant care, ecosystem dynamics, or your own gardening preferences. Consider how these lessons can guide you in future gardening endeavors.

Photos and Sketches: Attach or draw visual representations of your garden, specific plants, or notable moments. Visual elements can help you recall specific details and enhance your journal entries.

Bodily Wisdom over Intellectual Analysis
As other Moon gardening practitioners have told me, the key is to "get out of your own head." Overthinking is the antithesis of this practice. Rather, let your innate bodily wisdom take the lead, trusting your inner guide to navigate the complex web of interconnections between the Moon, the Earth and your own being.

FAMOUS GARDENERS WHO KEPT JOURNALS

Thomas Jefferson (1743-1826)- While not a gardener by profession, the third President of the United States was an avid horticulturist who maintained detailed garden journals for over 50 years. These journals contained records of planting dates, varieties and gardening techniques and are still studied today for their horticultural insight and historical importance.

Gertrude Jekyll (1843-1932)- An influential British horticulturist and garden designer, Gertrude Jekyll kept extensive notebooks and wrote many articles and books about gardening. Her work has been particularly influential in the area of planting design.

Luther Burbank (1849–1926) - An American botanist, horticulturist, and agricultural science pioneer, Burbank was responsible for more than 800 strains and varieties of plants, including the Russet Burbank potato. He kept detailed records of his plant breeding experiments, though these were more scientific logs than what might be thought of as a traditional garden journal. His meticulous record-keeping was crucial in developing new plant varieties.

Madame Ganna Walska (1887-1984) was an esteemed gardener known for her whimsical and eclectic design. She made scrapbooks of articles and photos that were her "mood boards" to get a feel for the garden she wanted to create. Much like an artist with a paint palette, she sought to follow her own style. Today, her Lotusland Garden in Montecito, California, remains celebrated for its careful curation and features over 3,000 plant species from around the world.

Closing Note:
The Art of Slowness when Moon Gardening

As we reach the final pages of this book, it's my hope that you've come to see Moon gardening as more than just a planting technique. It's an approach that encourages you to align your daily practices with the Moon's natural cycles, benefiting not only your garden but your holistic well-being. From discussions on good garden practices to the fine points of lunar planting, we've explored how this age-old wisdom can be both practical and profound in today's world.

Though the knowledge of natural cycles is deeply rooted in indigenous and traditional societies, it's crucial to remember that this wisdom is universal. The respect for nature and its cycles is a shared heritage that each of us can discover and appreciate, regardless of our cultural background. Far from being ancient relics, these traditions continue to enrich our lives, subtly influencing how we interact with our environment and ourselves.

Whether you've been cultivating a lush garden on sprawling land or nursing a modest herb garden on your city balcony, the principles of Moon gardening apply universally. Each plot of land, no matter its size, becomes a microcosm that reflects larger cosmic rhythms, filling your life with joy, relaxation and a sense of wonder.

By adhering to the Moon's phases in your gardening activities, you don't just nurture plants; you nurture a deeper understanding of yourself and your interconnectedness with the greater world. This book has been a journey through the hows and whys of Moon gardening, but it's also been a journey into understanding a way to slow down and live intentionally.

Thank you for embarking on this journey with me. Here's to many fruitful seasons ahead, guided by the Moon's gentle light.

Happy Moon Gardening,

The Supernature Team

Printed in Great Britain
by Amazon